ESSENTIAL GUITAR CHORDS
EVERYTHING YOU NEED TO PLAY BASIC GUITAR

JULIAN HAYMAN

GRAMERCY BOOKS
NEW YORK

This 2007 edition is published by Gramercy Books, an imprint of Random House Value Publishing, a division of Random House, Inc., New York, by arrangement with Amber Books.

Gramercy is a registered trademark and the colophon is a trademark of Random House, Inc.

Random House
New York • Toronto • London • Sydney • Auckland
www.randomhouse.com

Printed and bound in Dubai

A catalog record for this title is available from the Library of Congress.

ISBN: 978-0-517-22935-4

10 9 8 7 6 5 4 3 2

All photos and diagrams © Amber Books Ltd.

Contents

(ALTERNATIVE) = THIS WILL ENABLE YOU TO PLAY THE SAME CHORD, USING DIFFERENT FINGER POSITIONS.

Introduction

Essential guitar chords is the perfect tool for any aspiring guitar player or songwriter. These colorful chord charts are clear, easy-to-use and easy to understand.

Each section explains how to play the chord and is supported by a full-color diagram showing where to put your fingers on the strings. Each diagram is color-coded to illustrate the finger positions. A photograph is also featured to show the chord being played on the guitar.

This book features all of the popular major and minor chords from A–G which are used in a wide range of music, including rock, pop, folk and classical music. There are several ways to play each chord, so it is often a matter of deciding which is most comfortable for you, the guitarist. Some alternative fingerings are given for the most common chords.

Essential Guitar Chords is ideal for beginners and experienced players alike. Whether you are learning chords for the first time or simply need to refresh your memory, this book is an invaluable resource.

HOW THE CHORD DIAGRAMS WORK

The grey vertical rules are the guitar strings. The black horizontal rules are the frets. The frets are numbered from the nut (guitar neck) downwards.

The letters at the top of each string represent the open string note, starting with bottom E (the lowest string) on the left to the top E (the highest string) on the right.

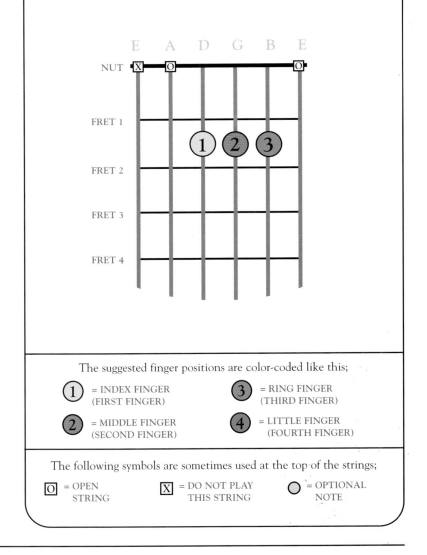

The suggested finger positions are color-coded like this;

① = INDEX FINGER (FIRST FINGER)

③ = RING FINGER (THIRD FINGER)

② = MIDDLE FINGER (SECOND FINGER)

④ = LITTLE FINGER (FOURTH FINGER)

The following symbols are sometimes used at the top of the strings;

O = OPEN STRING

X = DO NOT PLAY THIS STRING

◯ = OPTIONAL NOTE

A

A

Your index finger should play the 2nd fret of the D string, while your middle finger plays the 2nd fret of the G string and your ring finger plays the 2nd fret of the B string.

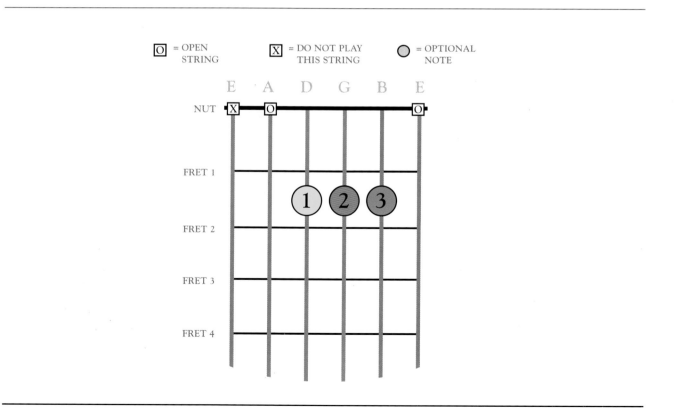

A (alt)

You can also play the A chord by using your index finger on the 5th frets
of the top E & B strings, your middle finger to play the 6th fret of the G string
and your ring finger to play the 7th fret of the D string.

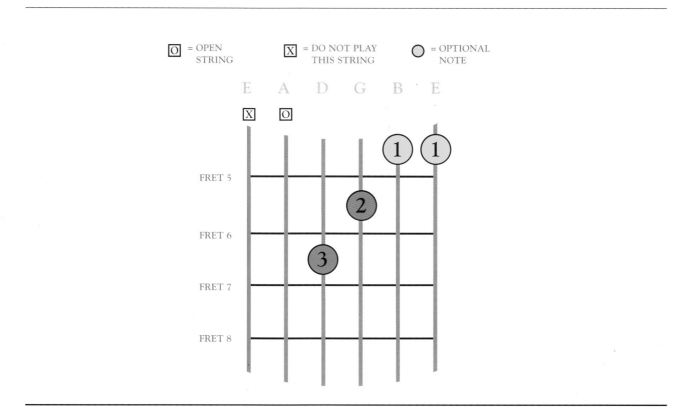

A7

Use your index finger across the 2nd frets of the top E, B, G & D strings only,
then use your middle or your ring finger, whichever feels most comfortable,
to play the G note at the 3rd fret of the top E string.

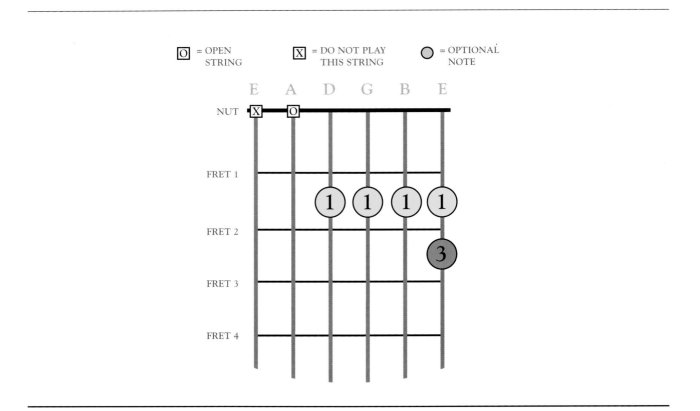

AM7

Use your index finger to play the 1st fret of the G string,
your middle finger to play the 2nd fret of the D string and finally
your ring finger to play the 2nd fret of the B string.

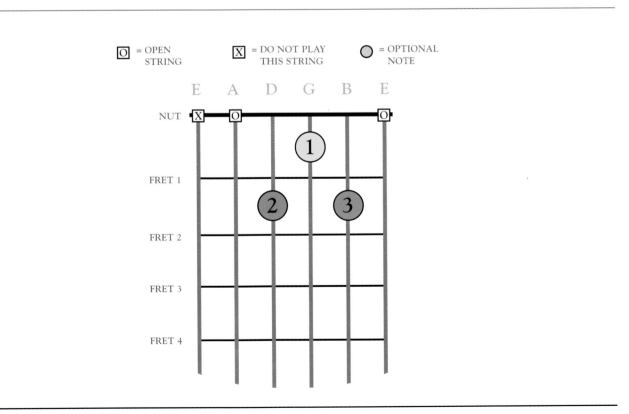

Am

Using your index finger play the C note at the 1st fret of the B string,
while your middle finger plays the 2nd fret of the D string
and your ring finger plays the 2nd fret of the G string.

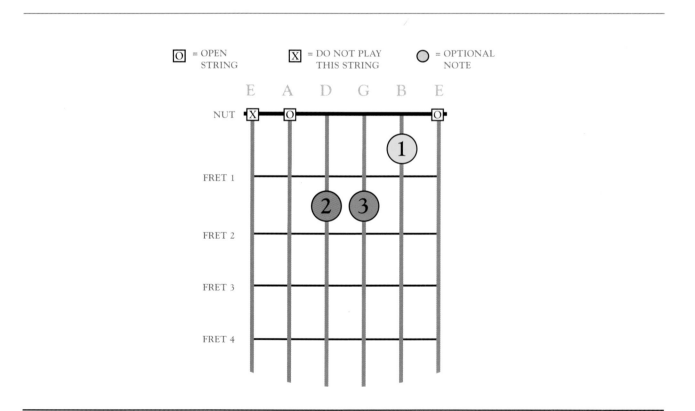

Am (alt)

Using your index finger play across all six strings of the 5th fret,
while your ring finger should play the 7th fret of the A string
and your little finger should play the 7th fret of the D string.

O = OPEN STRING X = DO NOT PLAY THIS STRING ◯ = OPTIONAL NOTE

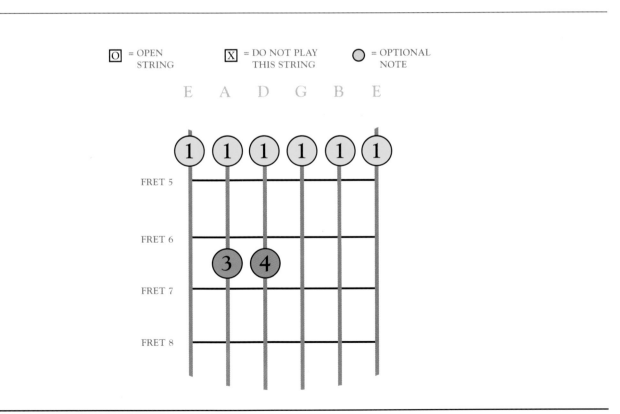

Am7

Let your index finger play the 1st fret of the B string and your middle finger the 2nd fret of the D string. You should play all the other strings, except the bottom E, open.

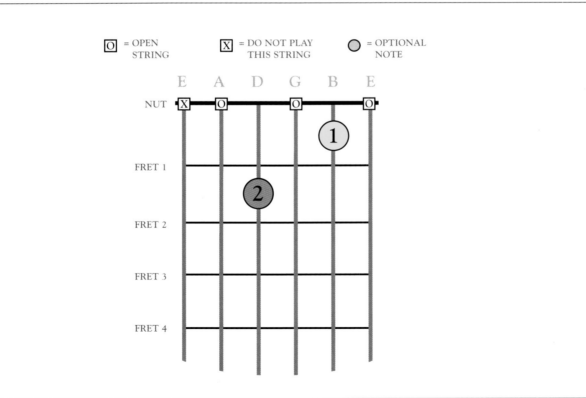

Use your index finger to play across the 2nd fret of the top E, B, G & D strings.

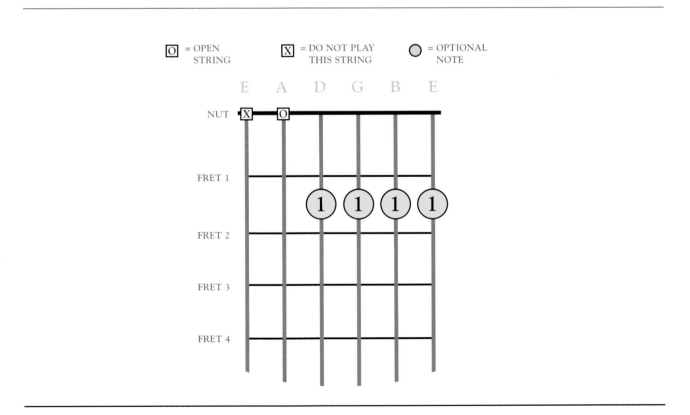

A9

Using your index finger, play across the 2nd fret of the top E, B, G & D strings,
while your middle finger plays the 3rd fret of the top E string
and your ring finger plays the 4th fret of the G string.

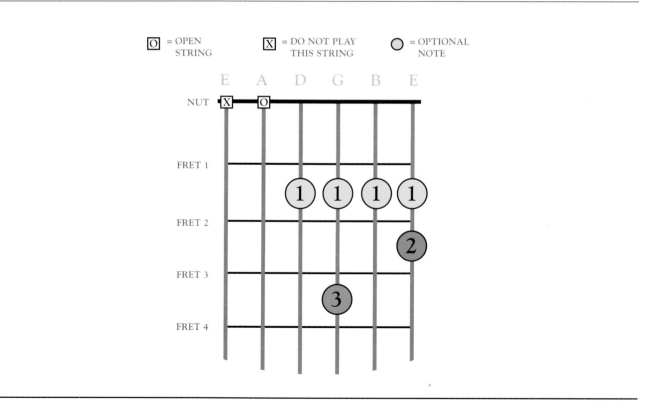

To play the chord of A flat, let your index finger play the 4th frets
of the B string & top E string, your middle finger play the 5th fret of the G string
and your ring finger play the 6th fret of the D string.

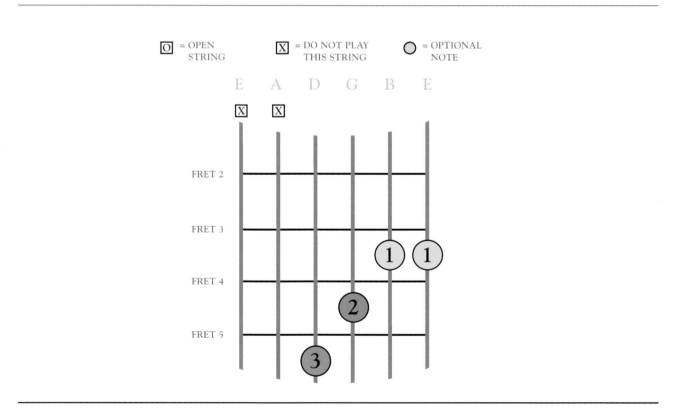

A♭(alt)

Let your index finger play the 6th fret of the D string,
your middle finger the 8th fret of the G string, your ring finger the 8th fret of the top E string
and your little finger the 9th fret of the B string.

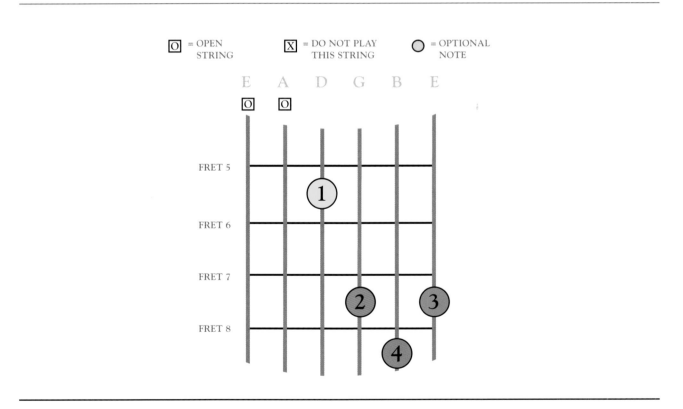

O = OPEN STRING   X = DO NOT PLAY THIS STRING   ◯ = OPTIONAL NOTE

E   A   D   G   B   E

FRET 5

FRET 6

FRET 7

FRET 8

Let your index finger play across the 4th frets of all the strings,
while your middle finger plays the 5th fret of the G string and your ring finger
plays the 6th fret of the A string.

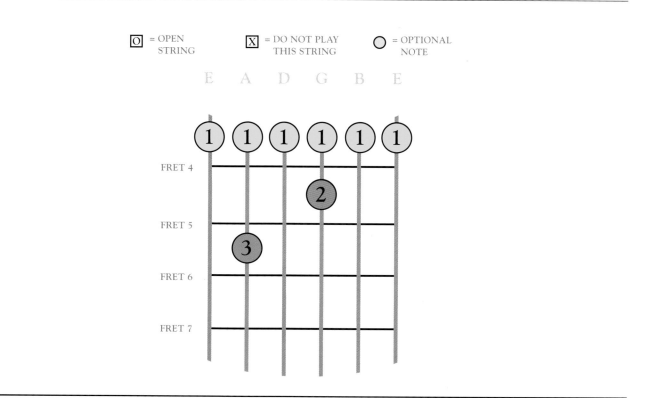

A♭M 7

Use your index finger to play the 3rd fret of the top E,
while your middle finger plays the 4th fret of the G string
and your little finger plays the 5th fret of the D string.

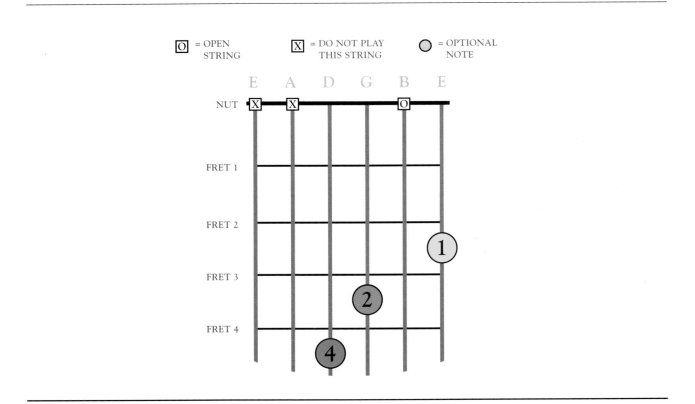

A♭m

Let your index finger play the 6th fret of the D string,
your middle finger the 7th fret of the top E string, your ring finger the 8th fret
of the G string and your little finger the 9th fret of the B string.

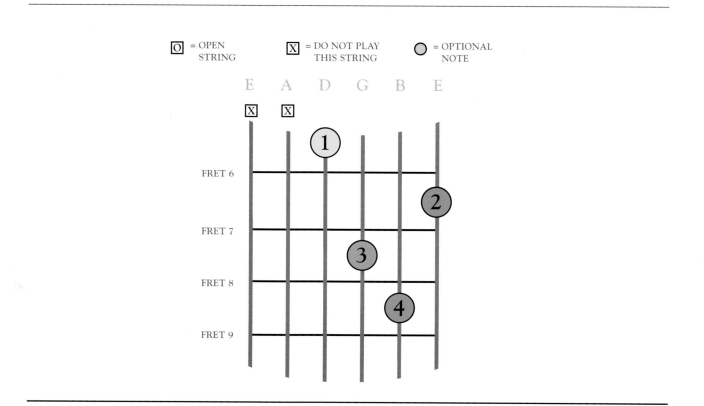

A♭m (alt)

Use your index finger to play across all six strings at the 4th fret.
Let your ring finger play 6th fret of the A string and your little finger
play the 6th fret of the D string.

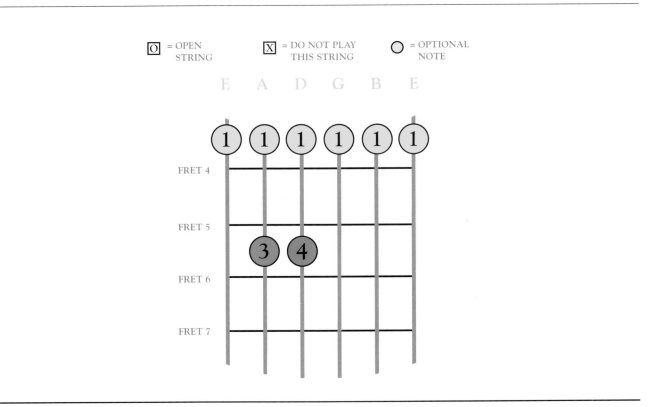

A♭m7

Let your index finger play across the 4th fret of every string,
while your middle finger plays the 6th fret of the A string, your ring finger the
6th fret of the D string and your little finger the 7th fret of the B string.

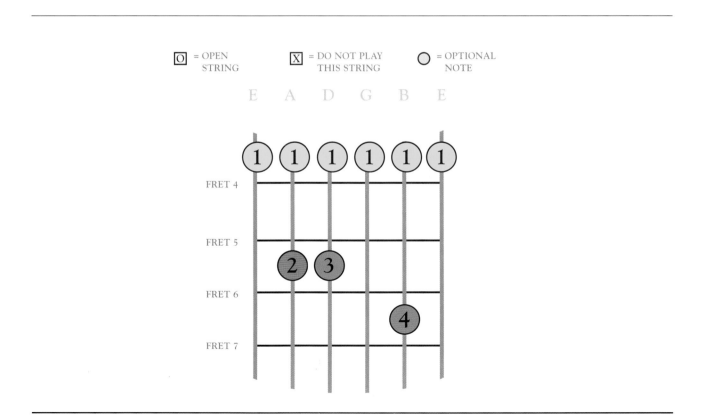

O = OPEN STRING   X = DO NOT PLAY THIS STRING   ◯ = OPTIONAL NOTE

E   A   D   G   B   E

FRET 4

FRET 5

FRET 6

FRET 7

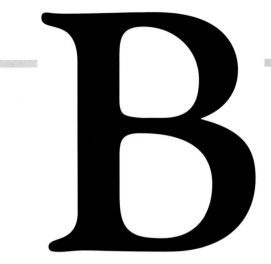

Let your index finger play the 2nd fret of the E, B, G, D & A strings.
Your middle finger plays the 4th fret of the D string, your ring finger the 4th fret of the G string
and your little finger the 4th fret of the B string.

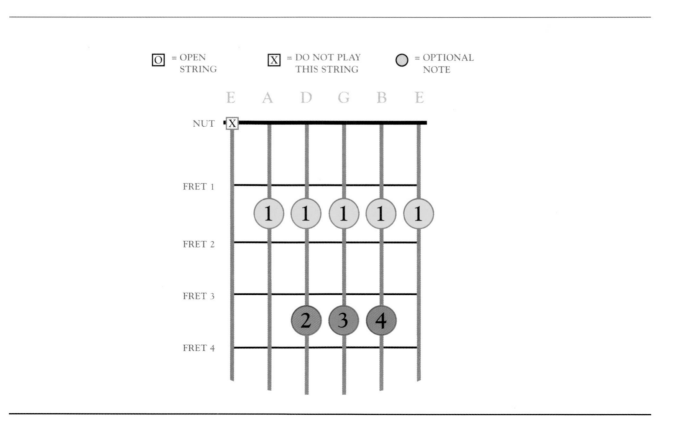

B (alt)

Your index finger should play the 7th fret of both the top E & B strings,
while your middle finger plays the 8th fret of the G string
and your ring finger plays the 9th fret of the D string.

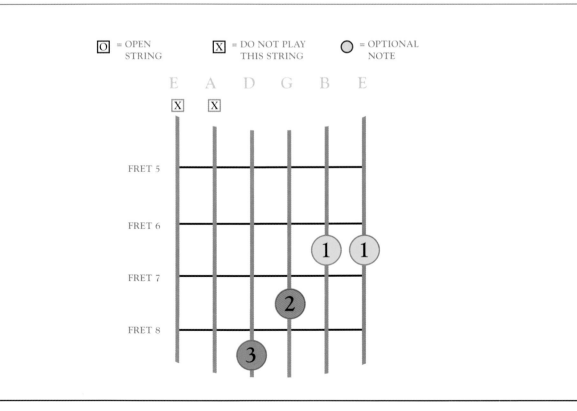

B7

Your index finger should play the 1st fret of the D string,
your middle finger the 2nd fret of the A string, your ring finger the 2nd fret of the G string
and your little finger the 2nd fret of the top E.

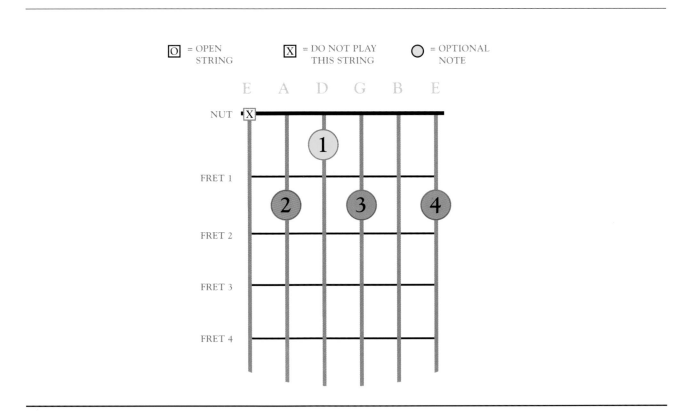

BM7

Cover the 2nd frets of the E, B, G, D & A strings with your index finger.
Your middle finger plays the 3rd fret of the G string, your ring finger the 4th fret of the D string
and your little finger the 4th fret of the B string.

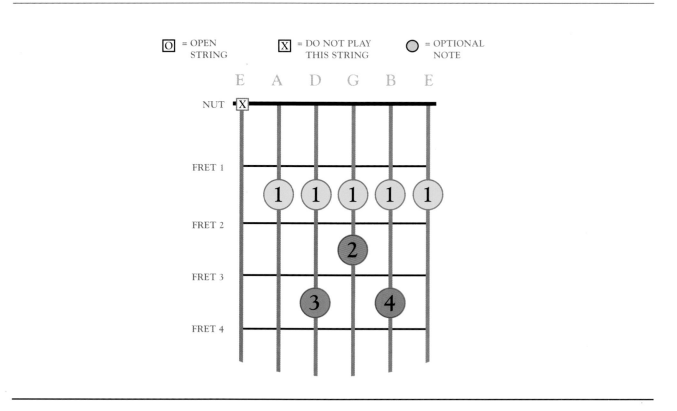

Using your index finger play across all six strings of the 7th fret,
while letting your ring finger play the 9th fret of the A string
and your little finger play the 9th fret of the D string.

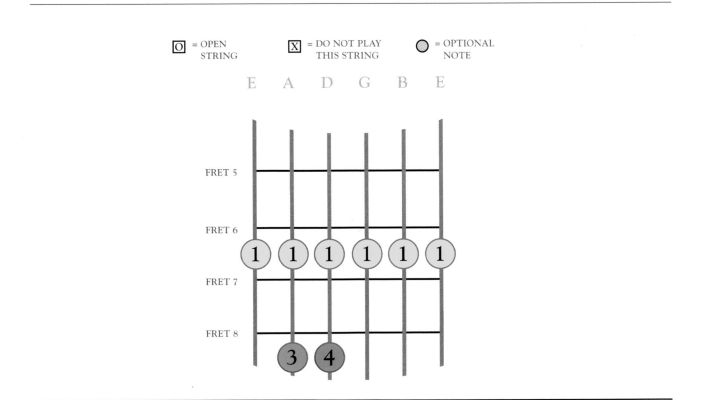

Bm (alt)

Let your index finger play the 2nd fret of the E, B, G, D & A strings,
your middle finger the 3rd fret of the B string, your ring finger the 4th fret of the D string
and your little finger the 4th fret of the G string

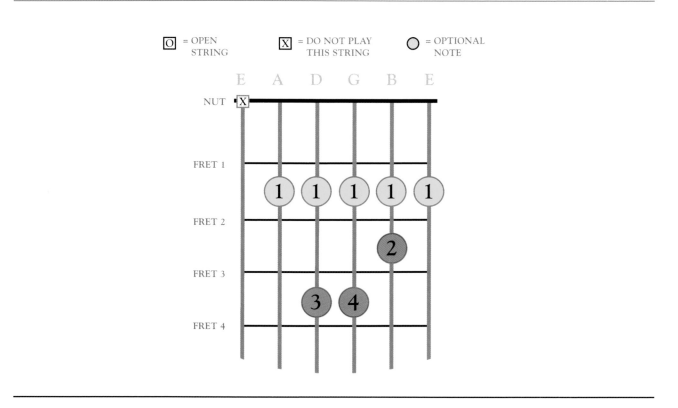

| ☐O = OPEN STRING | ☒X = DO NOT PLAY THIS STRING | ○ = OPTIONAL NOTE |

Bm7

Your index finger should play the 2nd fret of the A string, while your middle finger plays the 2nd fret of the G string and your ring finger the 2nd fret of the top E string.

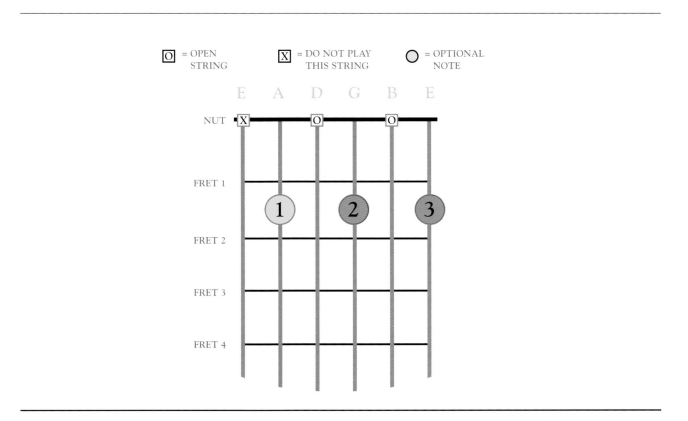

B♭

Let your index finger play the 1st fret of the top E string,
your middle finger the 3rd fret of the D string and your ring finger the 3rd fret of the G string,
then let your little finger play the 3rd fret of the B string.

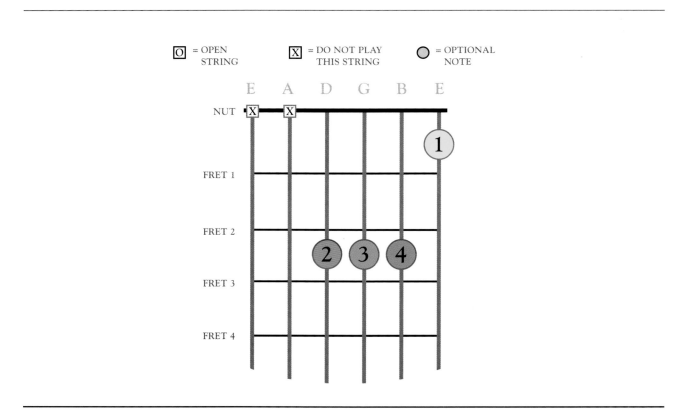

B♭ (alt)

Using your index finger play the 1st frets of the E, B, G, D & A strings,
while your middle finger plays the 3rd fret of the D string,
ring finger the 3rd fret of the G string and your little finger the 3rd fret of the B string.

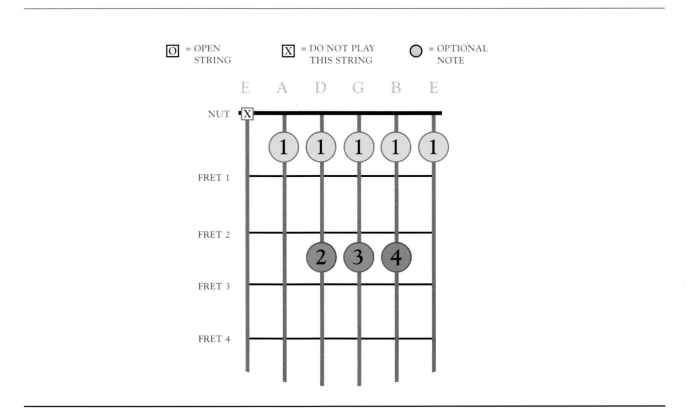

B♭7

Use your index finger to play across the 1st frets of the top E, B, G, D & A strings, then
your ring finger to play the 3rd fret of the D string and your little finger to play
the 3rd fret of the B string.

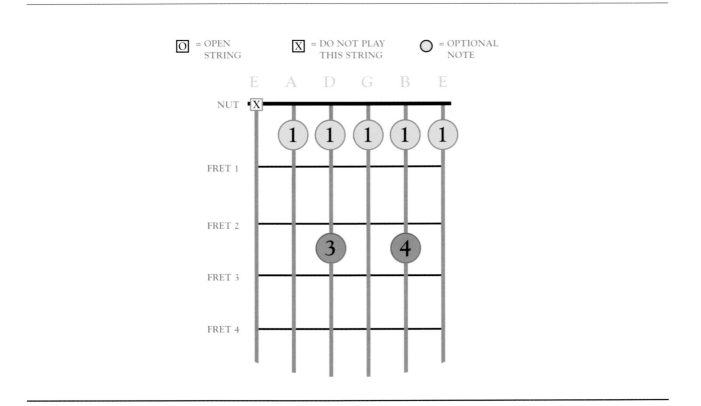

B♭M7

Your index finger covers the 1st frets of the E, B, G, D & A strings.
Your middle finger plays the 2nd fret of the G string, your ring finger the 3rd fret of the D string,
your little finger the 3rd fret of the B string.

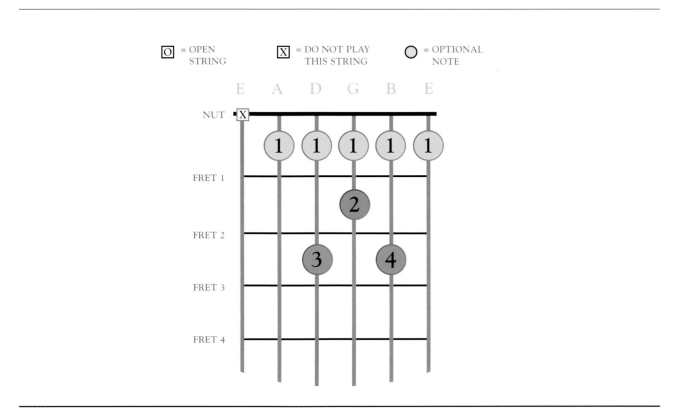

B♭m

Let your index finger play across all six strings of the 6th fret,
while your ring finger plays the 8th fret of the A string
and your little finger plays the 8th fret of the D string.

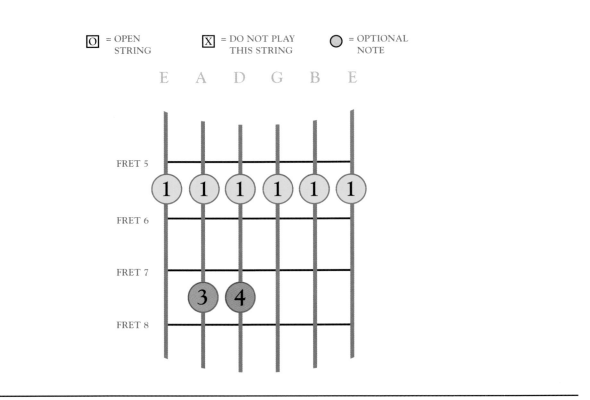

B♭m (alt)

Your index finger plays the E, B, G, D & A strings of the 1st fret,
your middle finger the 2nd fret of the B string, your ring finger the 3rd fret of the D string
and your little finger the 3rd fret of the G string.

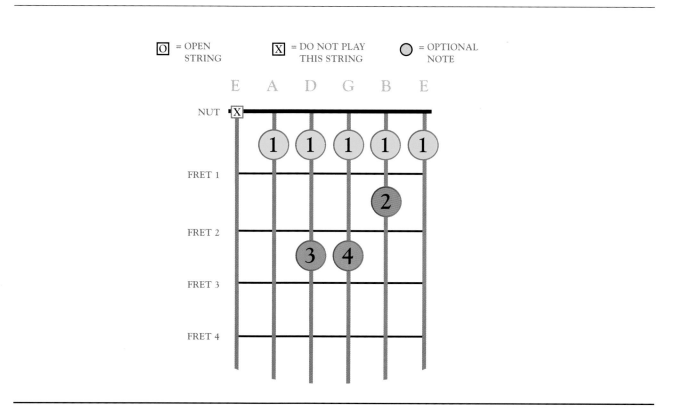

B♭m7

Using your index finger play the 1st fret of the top E, B, G, D & A strings,
while your middle finger plays the 2nd fret of the B string
and your ring finger the 3rd fret of the D string.

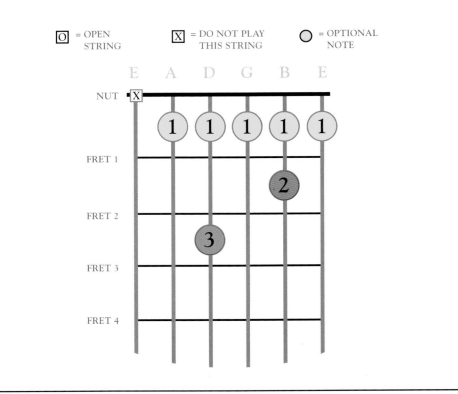

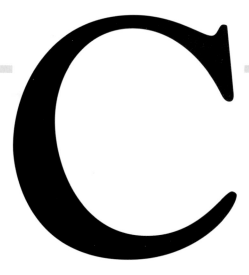

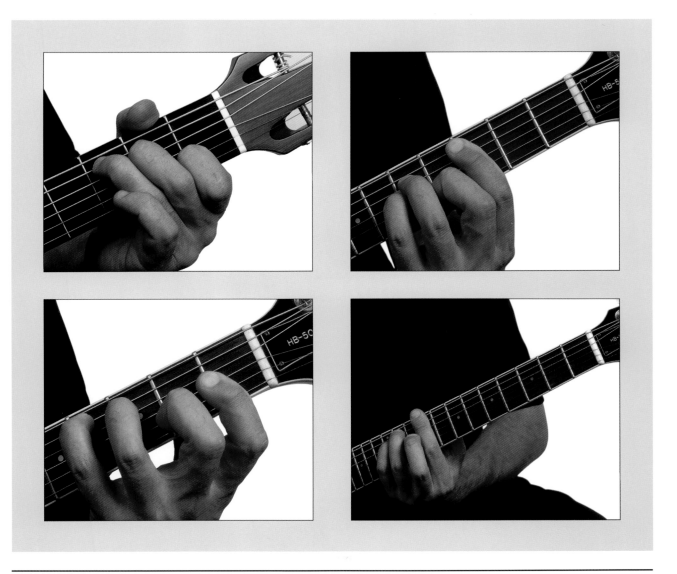

C

Your index finger should play the 1st fret of the B string, while your middle finger plays the 2nd fret of the D string and your ring finger the 3rd fret of the A string.

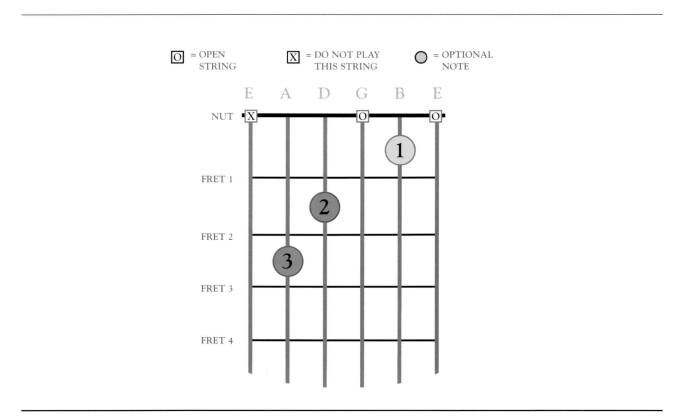

C (alt)

Let your index finger play the 3rd frets of the E, B, G, D & A strings,
your middle finger the 5th fret of the D string, your ring finger the 5th fret of the G string
and your little finger the 5th fret of the B string.

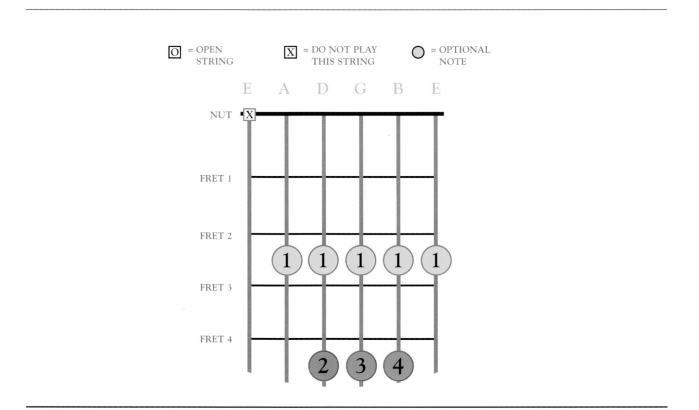

C7

Use your index finger to play the 1st fret of the B string,
your middle finger the 2nd fret of the D string, your ring finger the 3rd fret of the A string
and your little finger the 3rd fret of the G string.

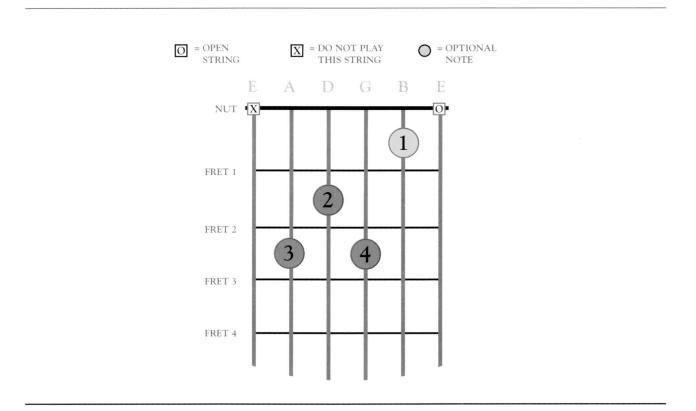

CM7

To play this chord you can use either your index and middle fingers
or your ring and little fingers – use whichever combination feels best.
Play the 2nd fret of the D string and the 3rd fret of the A string.

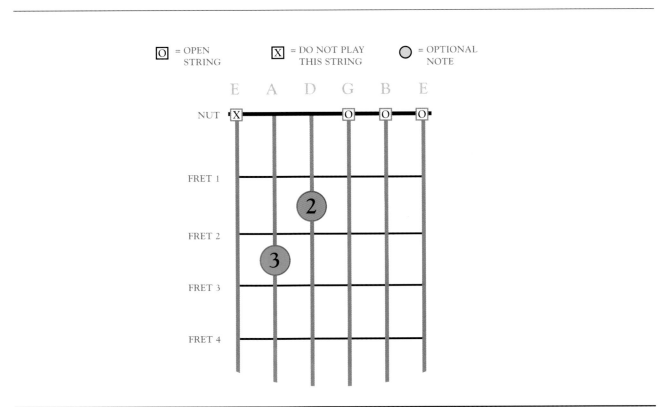

Cm

Your index finger plays the 3rd fret of the E, B, G, D & A strings,
your middle finger the 4th fret of the B string, your ring finger the 5th fret of the D string
and your little finger the 5th fret of the G string.

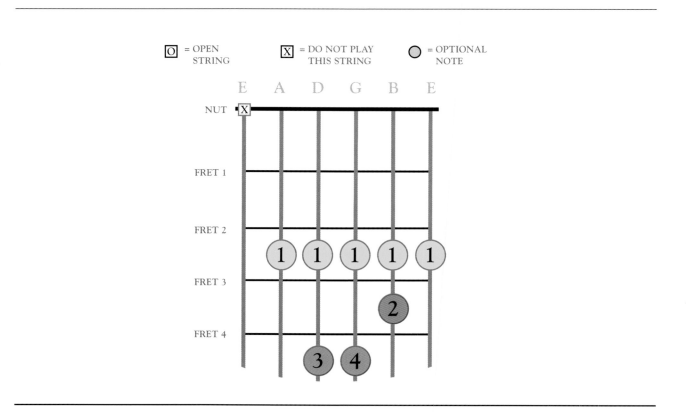

Cm (alt)

Using your index finger play across the 8th fret of all the strings,
while your ring finger plays the 10th fret of the A string
and your little finger plays the 10th fret of the D string.

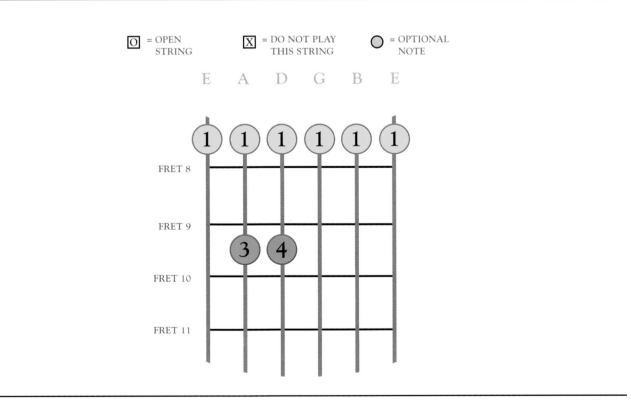

Cm7

Your index finger should cover the 3rd fret of
the top E, B, G, D & A strings, while your middle finger plays the 4th fret of the B string
and your ring finger the 5th fret of the D string.

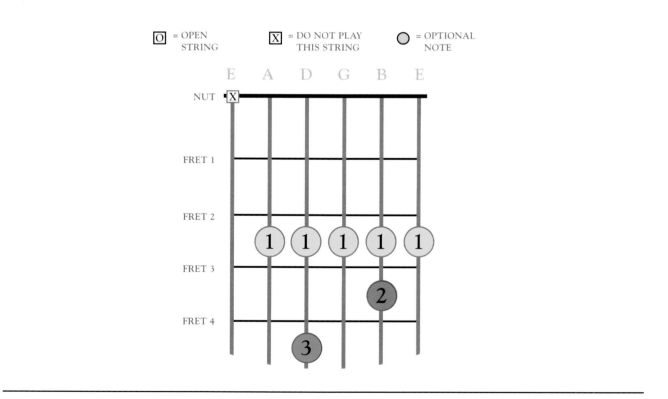

C6

Using your index finger play the 1st fret of the B string,
while your middle finger plays the 2nd fret of the D string, your ring finger the 2nd fret of the G string
and your little finger the 3rd fret of the A string.

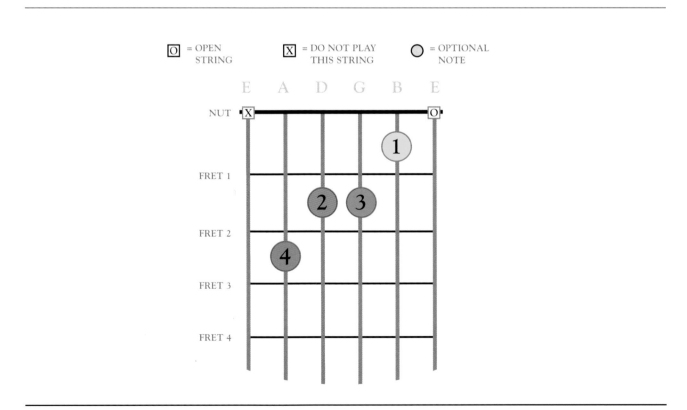

C9

Your index finger should play the 2nd fret of the D string,
your middle finger the 3rd fret of the A string, your ring finger the 3rd fret of the G string
and your little finger the 3rd fret of the B string.

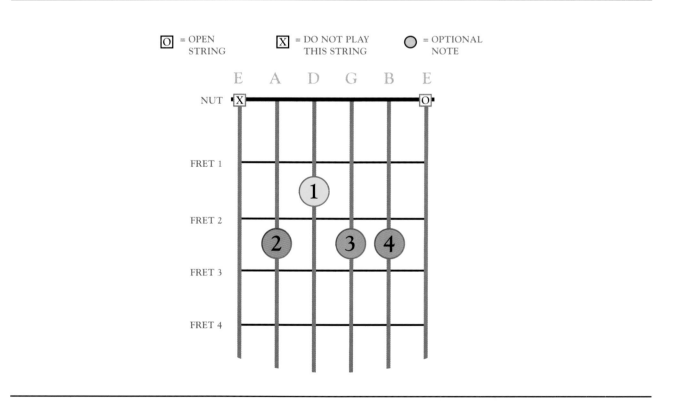

Let your index finger cover the 1st frets of the E, B & G strings.
Your middle finger plays the 2nd fret of the B string, your ring finger the 3rd fret of the D string
and your little finger the 4th fret of the A string.

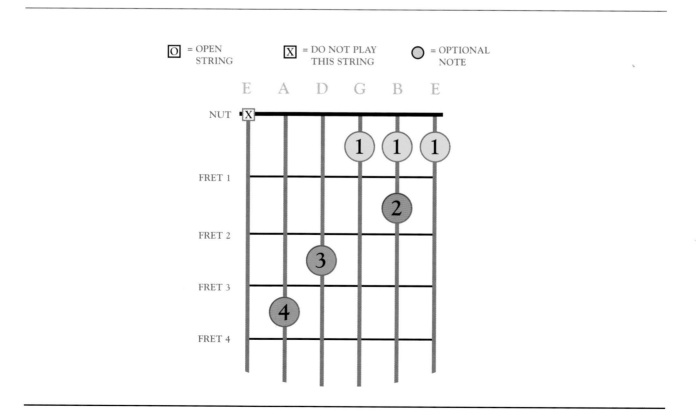

C[#] (alt)

Let your index finger cover the 4th frets of the E, B, G, D & A strings.
Your middle finger plays the 6th fret of the D string, your ring finger the 6th fret of the G string
and your little finger the 6th fret of the B string.

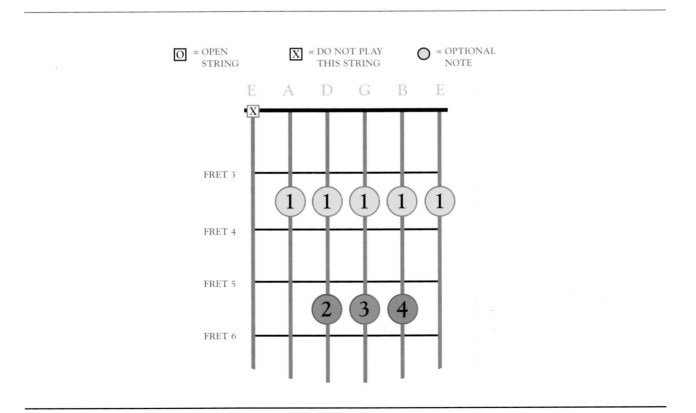

Use your index finger to play across the 4th frets of the E, B, G, D & A strings,
then use your ring finger to play the 6th fret of the D string
and your little finger to play the 6th fret of the B string.

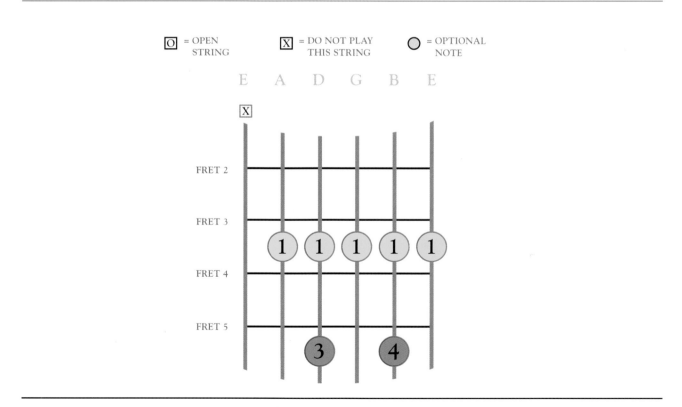

C#M7

Let your index finger play the 4th fret of the E, B, G, D & A strings.
Your middle finger plays the 5th fret of the G string, your ring finger the 6th fret of the D string
and your little finger the 6th fret of the B string.

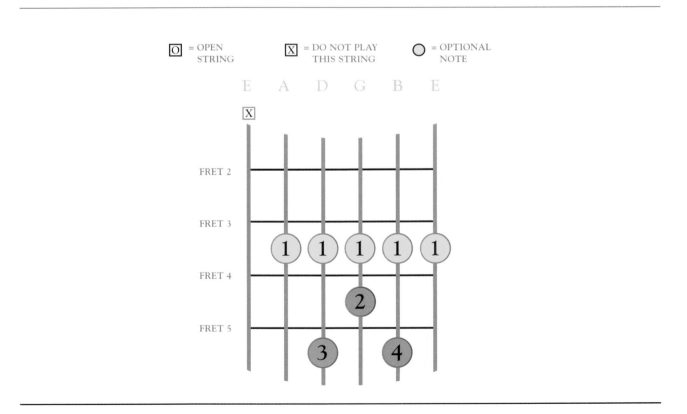

C#m

Let your index finger play the 4th fret of the top E, B, G, D & A strings,
your middle finger the 5th fret of the B string, your ring finger the 6th fret of the D string, your little finger
the 6th fret of the G string.

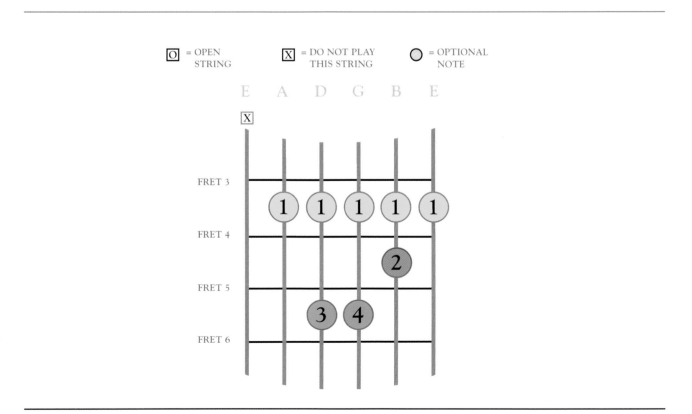

51

C#m (alt)

Using your index finger play across the 9th fret of all the strings,
while your ring finger plays the 11th fret of the A string
and your little finger plays the 11th fret of the D string.

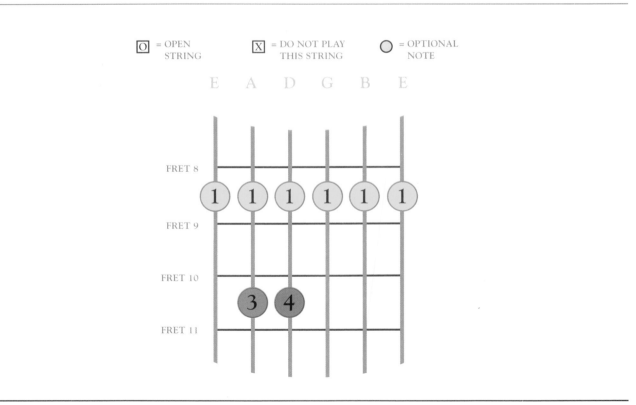

⊡ = OPEN STRING   ⊠ = DO NOT PLAY THIS STRING   ◯ = OPTIONAL NOTE

C#m7

Let your index finger cover the 4th fret of the top E, B, G, D & A strings,
while your middle finger plays the 5th fret of the B string
and your ring finger the 6th fret of the D string.

O = OPEN STRING   X = DO NOT PLAY THIS STRING   ◯ = OPTIONAL NOTE

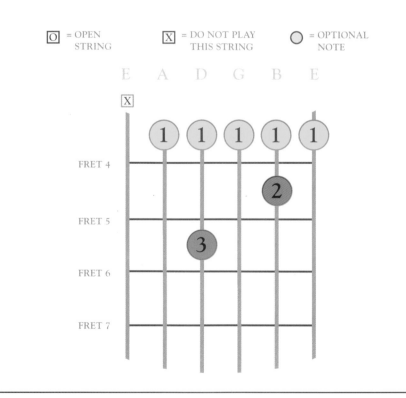

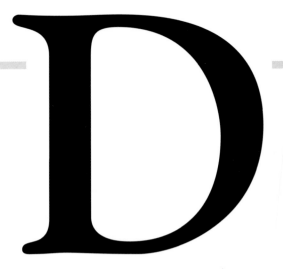

Your index finger should play the 2nd fret of the G string,
while your middle finger plays the 2nd fret of the top E
and your ring finger plays the 3rd fret of the B string.

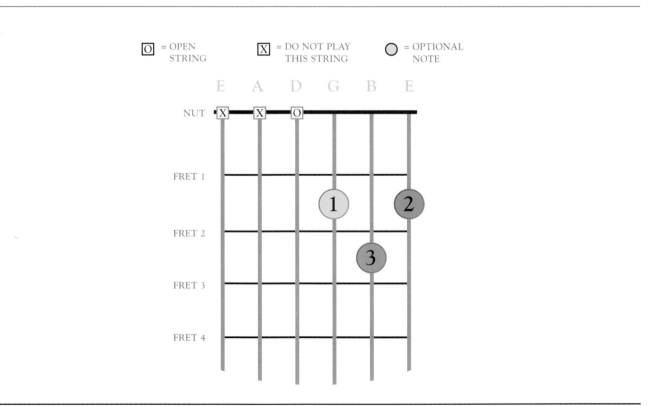

D (alt)

Your index finger should play the 5th fret of the top E string,
your middle finger the 7th fret of the D string, your ring finger the 7th fret of the G string
and your little finger the 7th fret of the B string.

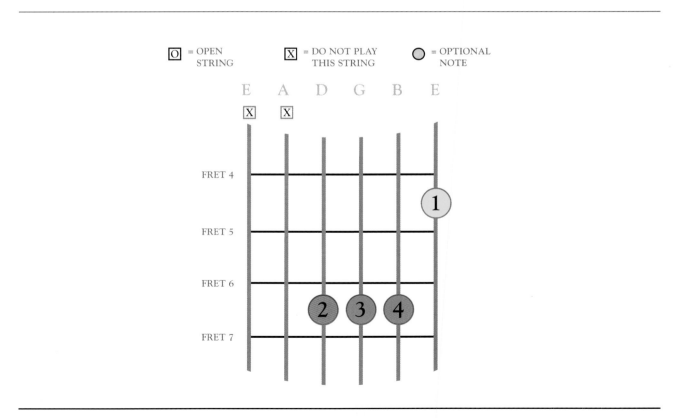

D7

Let your index finger play the 1st fret of the B string,
while your middle finger should play the 2nd fret of the G string
and finally your ring finger plays the 2nd fret of the top E string.

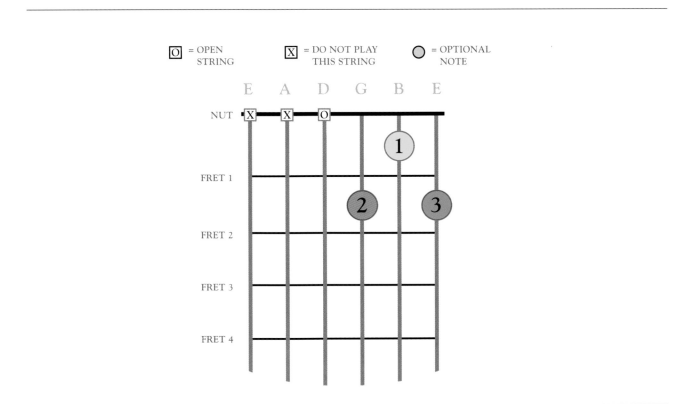

DM7

THE D CHORD FAMILY

D major 7

Let your index finger play the 5th fret of the E, B, G, D & A strings,
your middle finger the 6th fret of the G string, your ring finger the 7th fret of the D string
and your little finger the 7th fret of the B string.

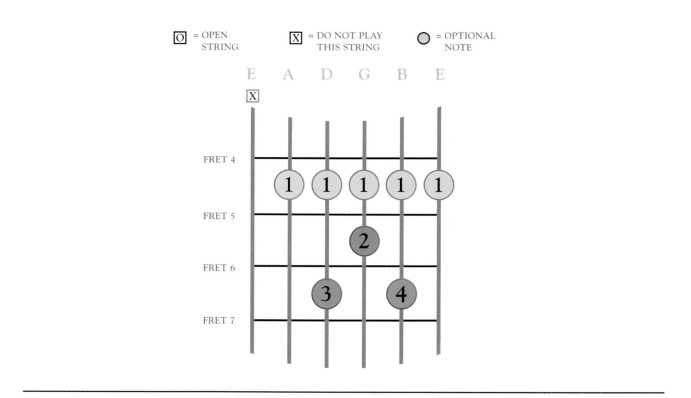

Dm

Let your index finger play the 1st fret of the top E string,
while your middle finger plays the 2nd fret of the G string
and your ring finger plays the 3rd fret of the B string.

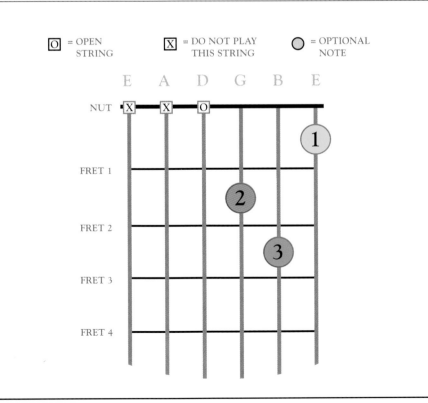

Dm (alt)

Let your index finger play the 5th fret of the E, B, G, D & A strings,
your middle finger the 6th fret of the B string, your ring finger the 7th fret of the D string
and your little finger the 7th fret of the G string.

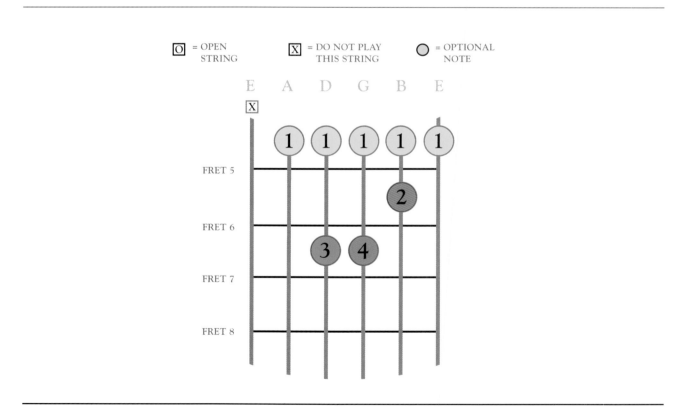

Dm7

Using your index finger play the 1st fret of the top E & the B strings,
and let your middle finger play the 2nd fret of the G string, including the D string,
which is played open.

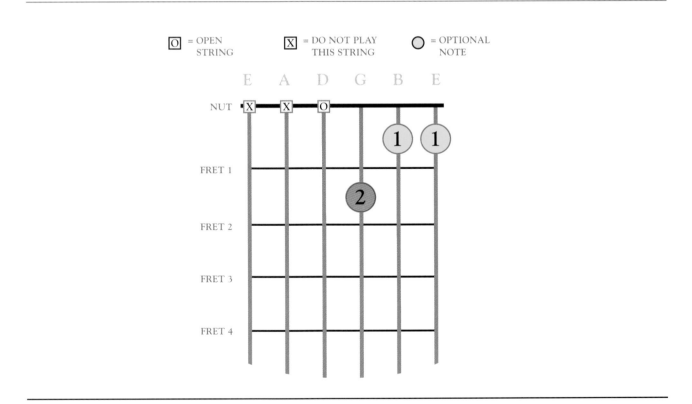

D6

For this chord you can use either your index and middle fingers,
or your middle and ring fingers, to play the
2nd fret of the G string and the top E string.

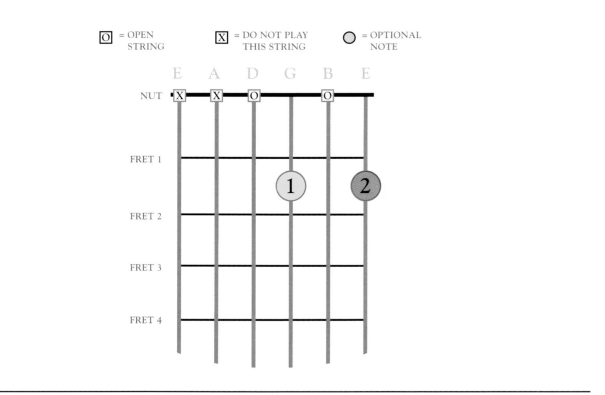

D9

This is an easy one! Let your index finger play the 1st fret of the B string
and your middle finger play the 2nd fret of the G string.
The D string and the top E string should be played open.

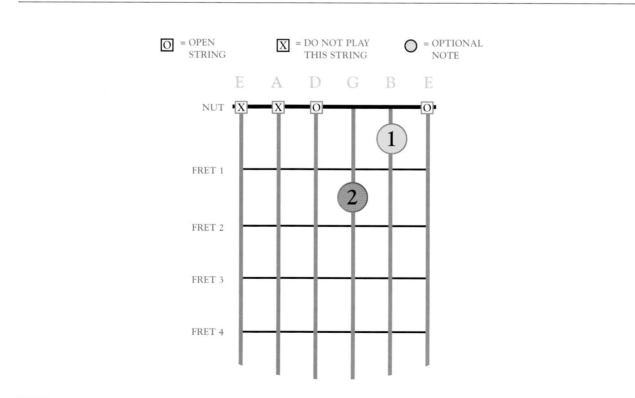

E

E

For the E chord your index finger should play the 1st fret of the G string,
while your middle finger plays the 2nd fret of the A string
and your ring finger the 2nd fret of the D string.

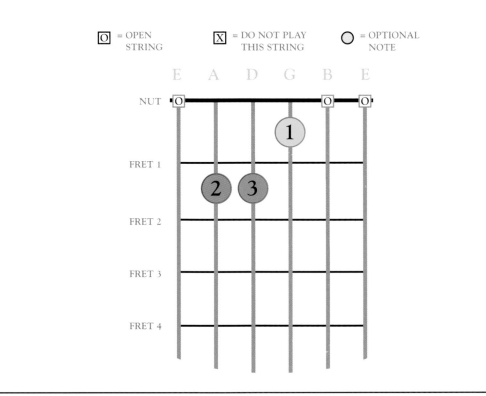

E (alt)

Let your index finger play the 2nd fret of the D string,
your middle finger the 4th fret of the G string, your ring finger the 4th fret of the top E string
and your little finger the 5th fret of the B string.

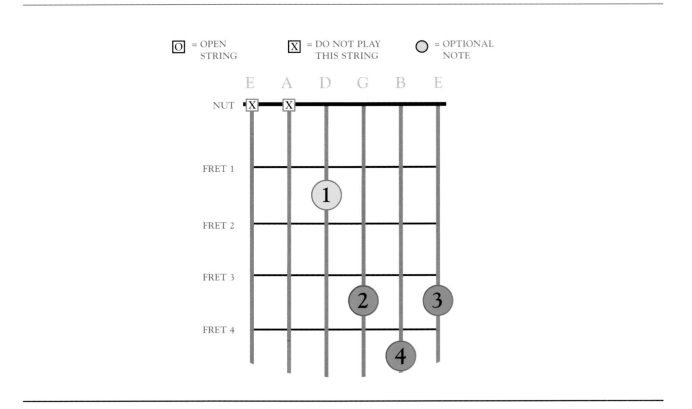

E7

Let your index finger play the 1st fret of the G string,
while your middle finger plays the 2nd fret of the A string,
your ring finger the 2nd fret of the D string and your little finger the 3rd fret of the B string.

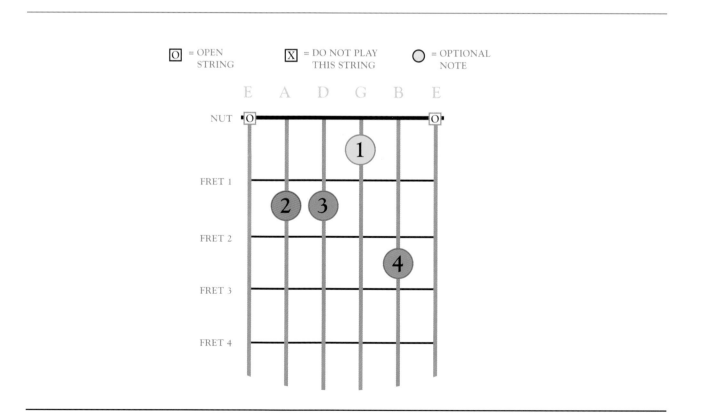

EM7

Using your index finger play the 1st fret of the D string,
while your middle finger plays the 1st fret of the G string
and finally your ring finger plays the 2nd fret of the A string.

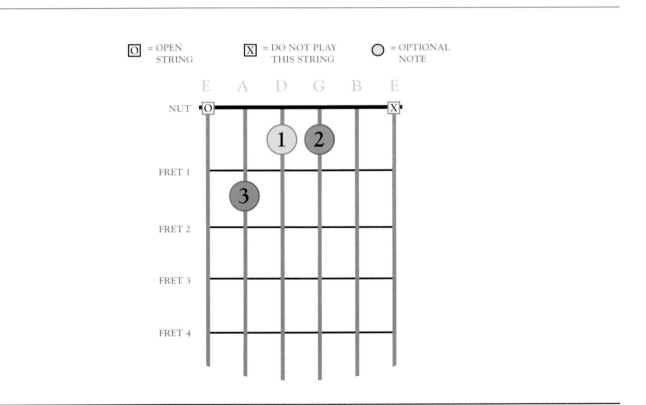

68

Em

Your index finger should play the 2nd fret of the A string,
while your middle finger plays the 2nd fret of the D string.
You can use the middle and ring fingers instead, if that feels more comfortable.

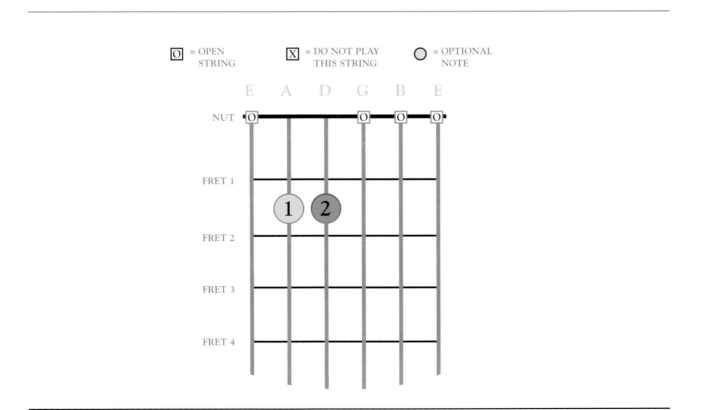

Em (alt)

Let your index finger play the 7th fret of the E, B, G, D & A strings,
your middle finger the 8th fret of the B string, your ring finger the 9th fret of the D string
and your little finger the 9th fret of the G string.

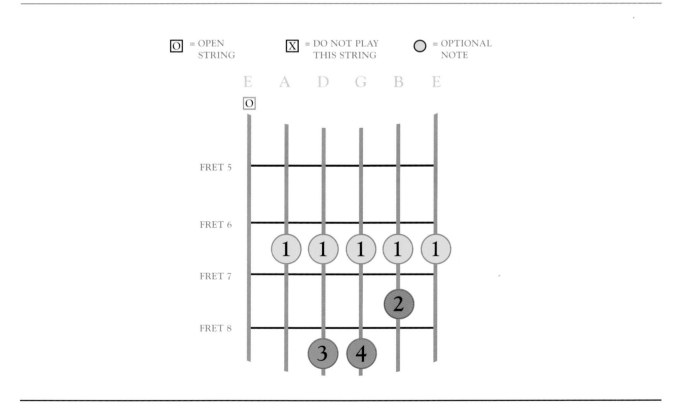

Em7

Your index finger should play the 2nd fret of the A string,
while your middle finger plays the 2nd fret of the D string
and your ring or little finger plays the 3rd fret of the B string.

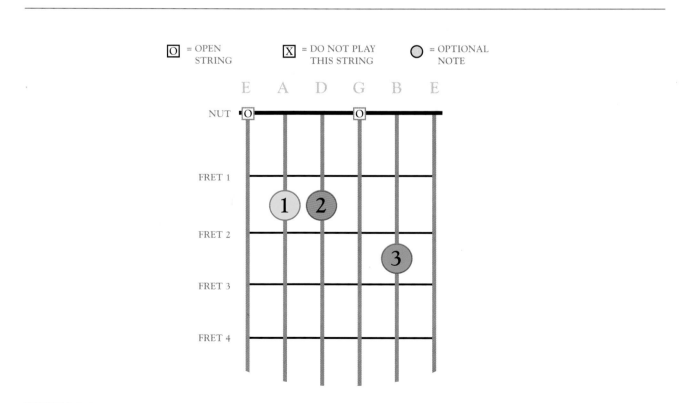

E6

Let your index finger play the 1st fret of the G string,
your middle finger the 2nd fret of the A string, your ring finger plays the 2nd fret of the D string,
and your little finger should play the 2nd fret of the B string.

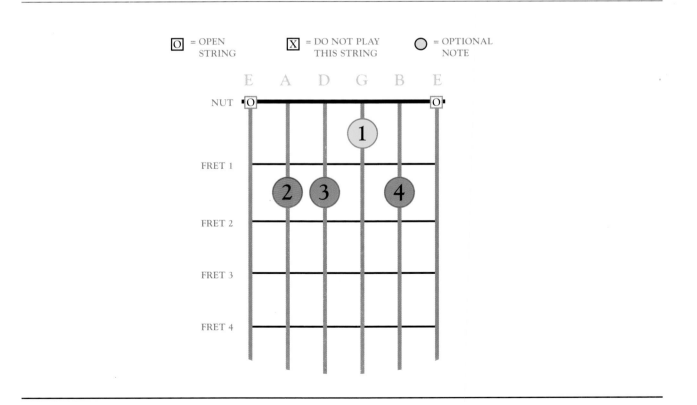

E9

Using your index finger play the 1st fret of the G string,
while your middle finger plays the 2nd fret of the A string
and your ring finger plays the 2nd fret of the top E string.

O = OPEN STRING   X = DO NOT PLAY THIS STRING   O = OPTIONAL NOTE

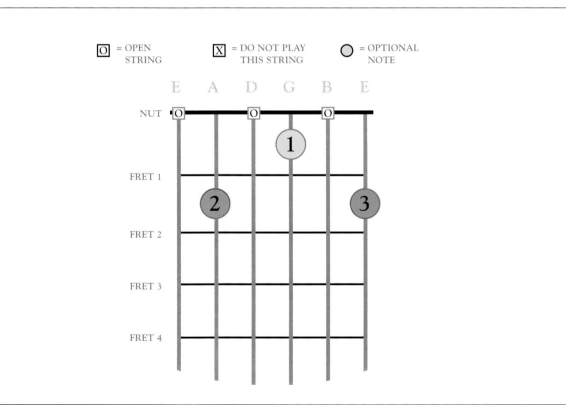

E♭

Your index finger should play the 1st fret of the D string,
your middle finger the 3rd fret of the G string, your ring finger the 3rd fret of the top E string
and your little finger the 4th fret of the B string.

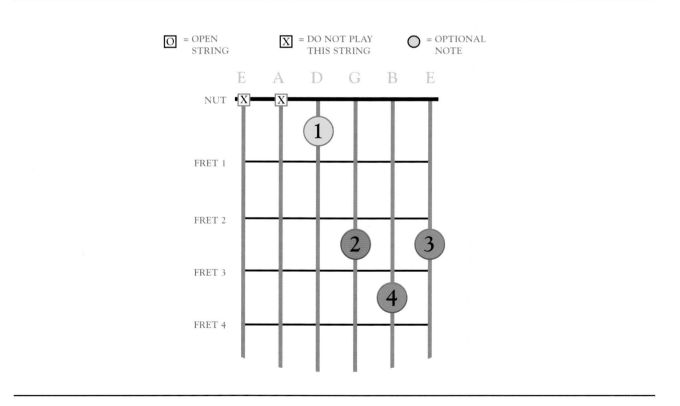

E♭ (alt)

Your index finger covers the 3rd fret of the E, B & G strings,
while your middle finger plays the 4th fret of the B string,
your ring finger the 5th fret of the D string and your little finger the 6th fret of the A string.

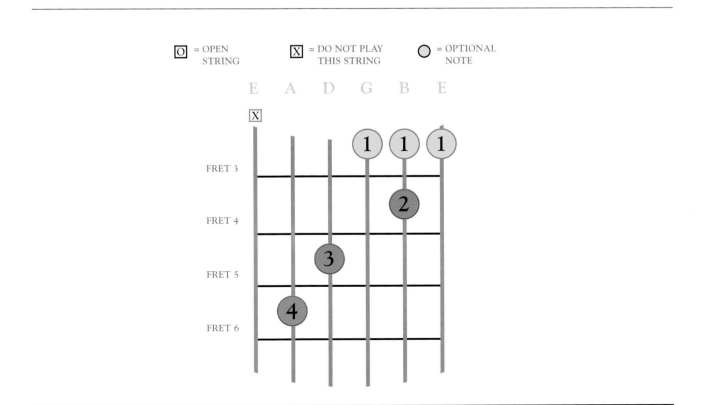

E♭7

Let your index finger play the 1st fret of the D string,
your middle finger the 2nd fret of the B string, your ring finger the 3rd fret of the G string
and your little finger the 3rd fret of the top E string.

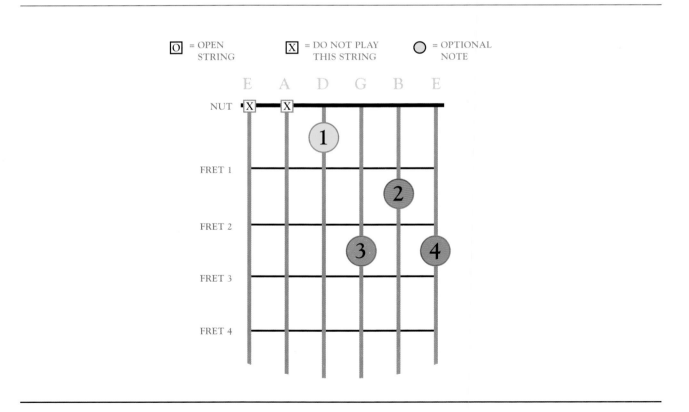

E♭M7

Using your index finger play the 1st fret of the D string,
then let your ring finger (or middle finger if that feels more comfortable)
cover the 3rd fret of the top E, B & G strings.

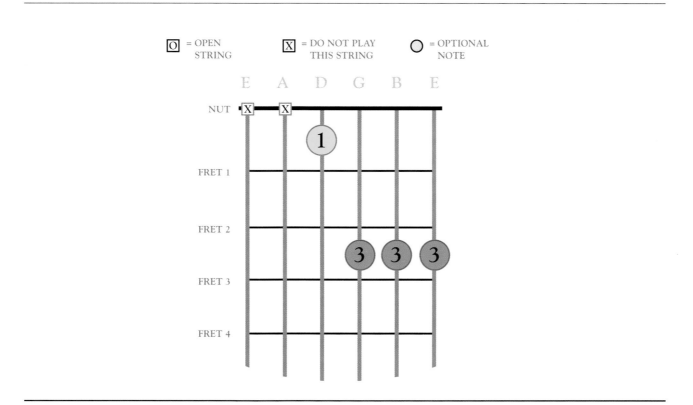

E♭m

Let your index finger play the 1st fret of the D string,
while your middle finger plays the 2nd fret of the top E string,
your ring finger the 3rd fret of the G string and your little finger the 4th fret of the B string.

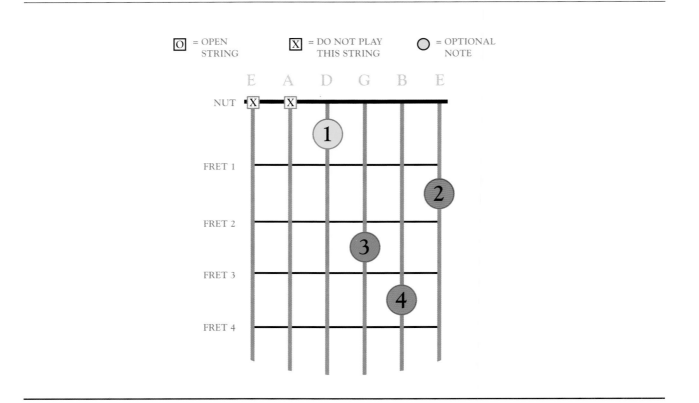

E♭m (alt)

Let your index finger play the 6th fret of the E, B, G, D & A strings,
your middle finger the 7th fret of the B string, your ring finger the 8th fret of the D string
and your little finger the 8th fret of the G string.

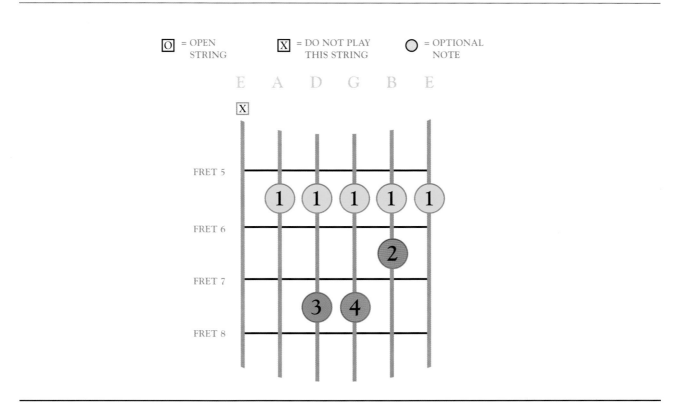

E♭m7

Using your index finger play the 1st fret of the D string,
your middle finger plays the 2nd fret of the B string, your ring finger the 2nd fret of the top E string
and finally your little finger the 3rd fret of the G string.

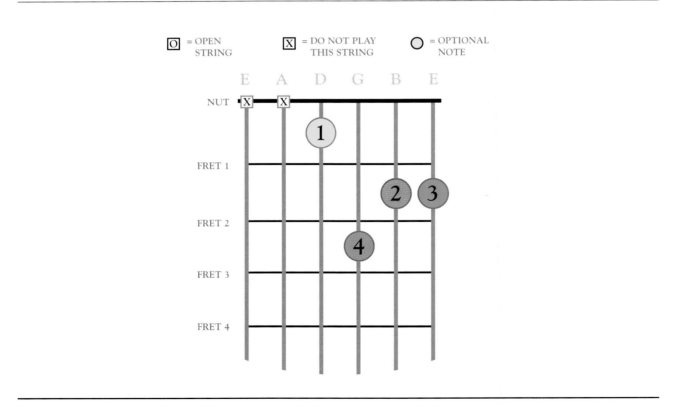

F

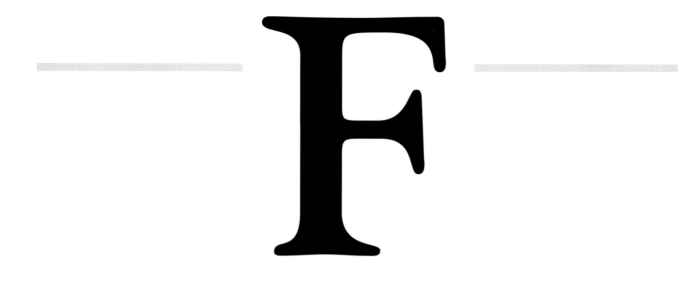

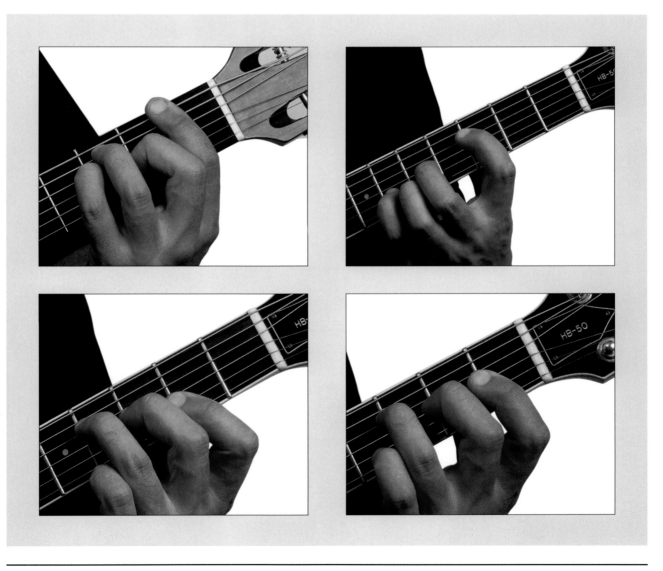

F

Your index finger should play the 1st fret of the top E & B strings,
while your middle finger plays the 2nd fret of the G string
and your ring finger the 3rd fret of the D string.

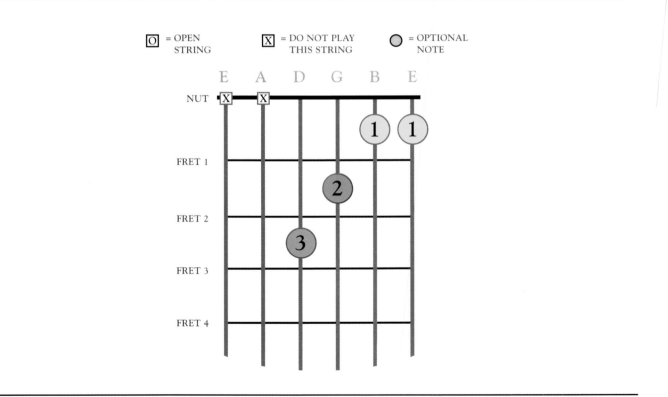

F(alt)

Let your index finger play the 3rd fret of the D string,
your middle finger the 5th fret of the G string,
your ring finger the 5th fret of the top E string and your little finger the 6th fret of the B string.

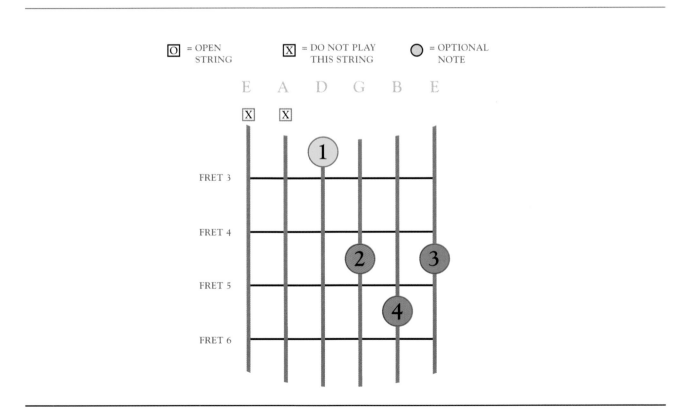

F Bar

Let your index finger play the 1st fret of all the strings,
while your middle finger plays the 2nd fret of the G string,
your ring finger the 3rd fret of the A string and your little finger the 3rd fret of the D string.

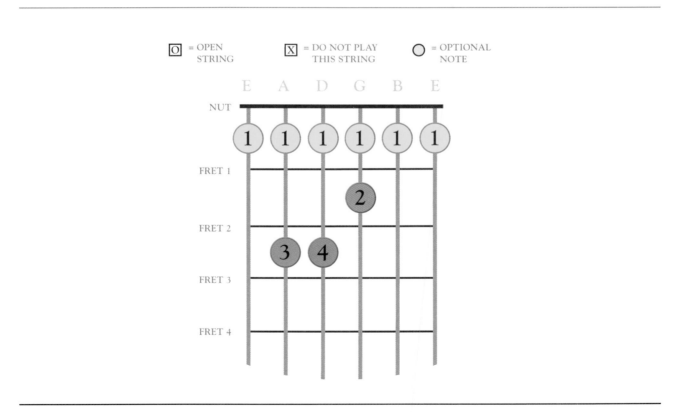

F7

Let your index finger play across the 1st fret of all the strings,
while your middle finger plays the 2nd fret of the G string
and your ring finger plays the 3rd fret of the A string.

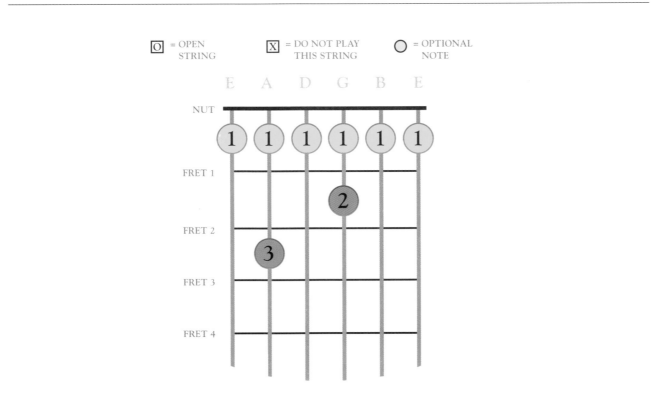

O = OPEN STRING   X = DO NOT PLAY THIS STRING   ◯ = OPTIONAL NOTE

FM7

Your index finger should play the 1st fret of the B string,
while your middle finger should play the 2nd fret of the G string
and your ring finger should play the 3rd fret of the D string.

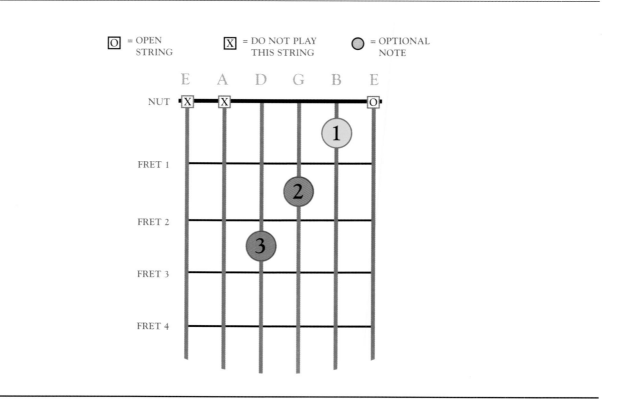

Fm

Let your index finger play the 3rd fret of the D string,
while your middle finger plays the 4th fret of the top E string,
your ring finger the 5th fret of the G string and your little finger the 6th fret of the B string.

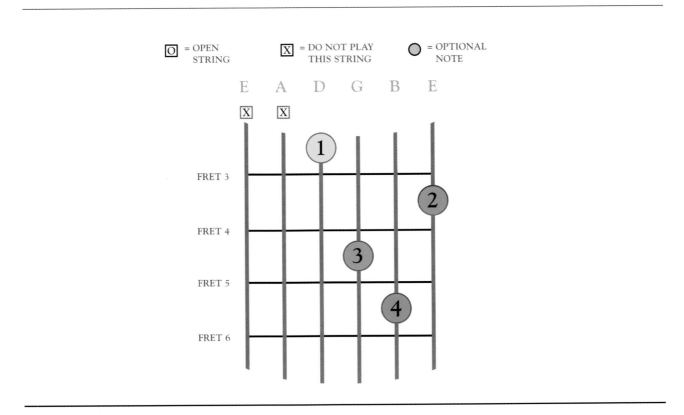

Fm (alt)

Your index finger should play the 1st fret of all the strings,
while your ring finger should play the 3rd fret of the A string
and your little finger should play the 3rd fret of the D string.

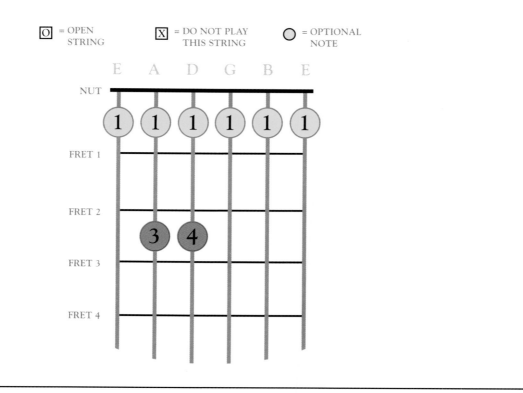

Fm7

Let your index finger play the 1st fret of all the strings,
your middle finger the 3rd fret of the A string, your ring finger the 3rd fret of the D string
and your little finger the 4th fret of the B string.

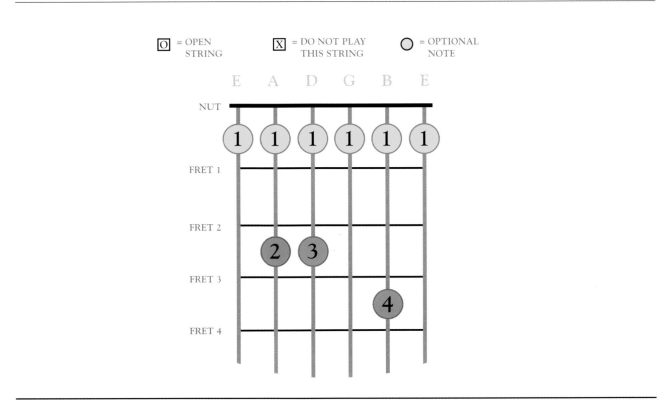

Fm Bar

Using your index finger play the 1st fret of all six strings,
while your ring finger should play the 3rd fret of the A string
and your little finger should play the 3rd fret of the D string.

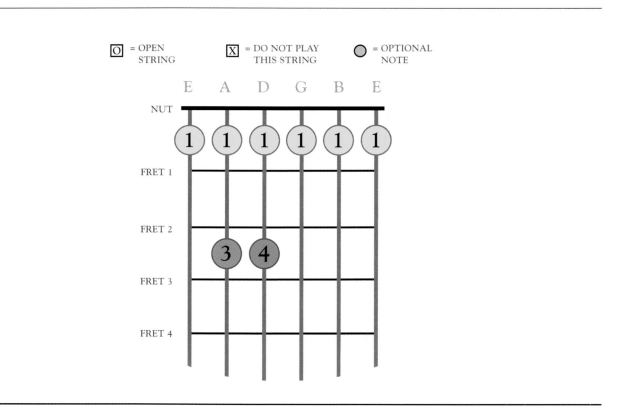

Your index finger should play the 1st fret of the top E string,
your middle finger the 2nd fret of the G string, your ring finger the 3rd fret of the D string
and your little finger the 3rd fret of the B string.

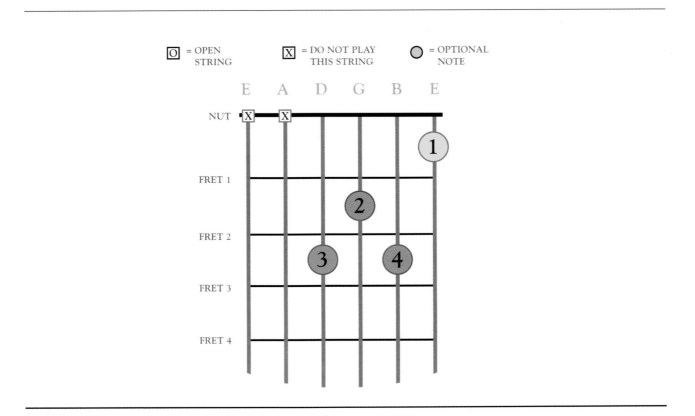

F9

Let your index finger play the 1st fret of all six strings,
your middle finger the 2nd fret of the G string, your ring finger the 3rd fret of the A string
and your little finger the 3rd fret of the top E string.

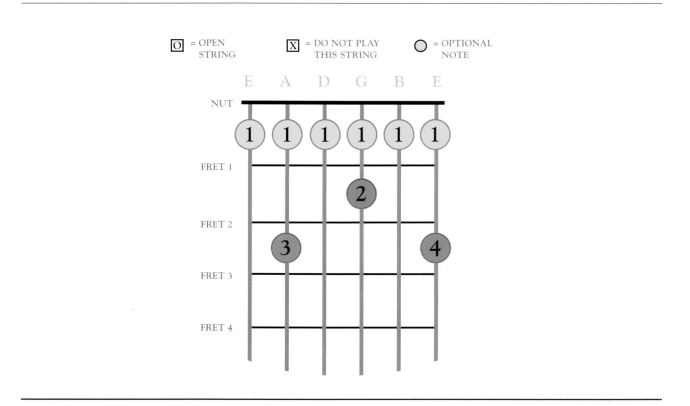

For the F# chord use your index finger to play the 2nd fret of the top E & B strings,
while your middle finger plays the 3rd fret of the G string
and your ring finger plays the 4th fret of the D string

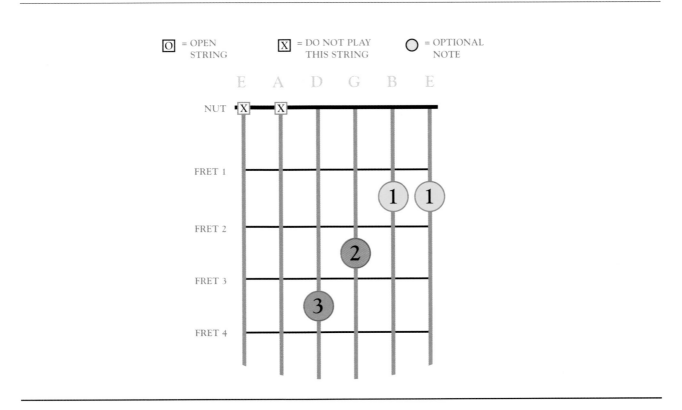

O = OPEN STRING X = DO NOT PLAY THIS STRING O = OPTIONAL NOTE

F#(alt)

Let your index finger play the 4th fret of the D string,
your middle finger the 6th fret of the G string,
your ring finger the 6th fret of the top E string and your little finger the 7th fret of the B string.

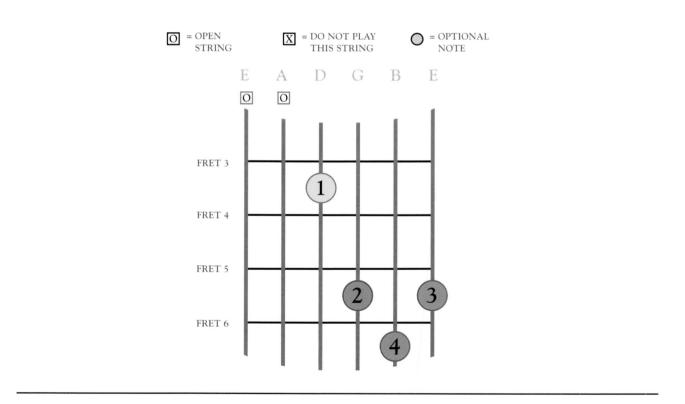

F#7

Let your index finger play across the 2nd fret of all the strings,
while your middle finger plays the 3rd fret of the G string
and your ring finger plays the 4th fret of the A string.

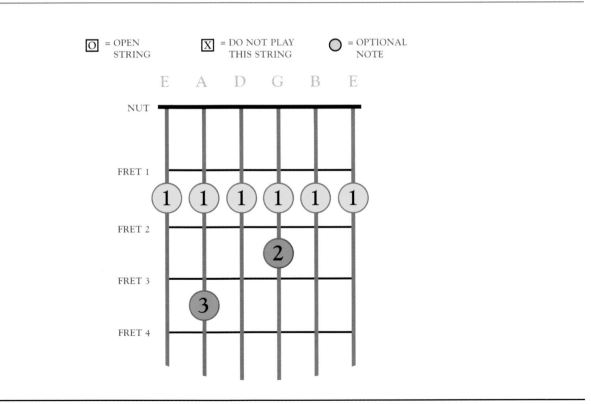

F#M7

Let your index finger play the 1st fret of the top E string,
your middle finger the 2nd fret of the B string, your ring finger the 3rd fret of the G string
and your little finger the 4th fret of the D string.

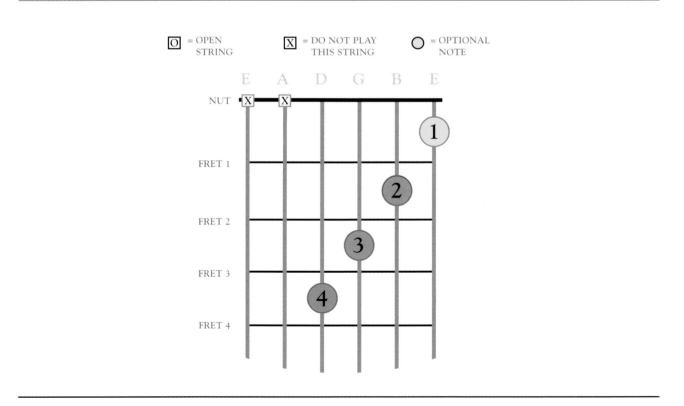

F#m

Let your index finger play the 4th fret of the D string,
your middle finger the 5th fret of the top E string, your ring finger the 6th fret of the G string
and your little finger the 7th fret of the B string.

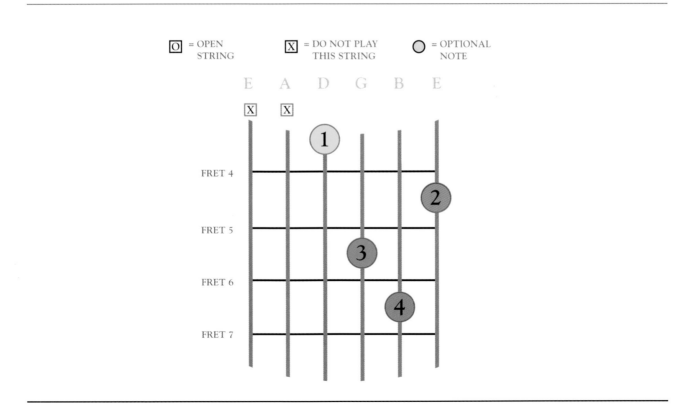

F#m (alt)

Using your index finger play the 2nd fret of all six strings.
Your ring finger should play the 4th fret of the A string
and your little finger should play the 4th fret of the D string.

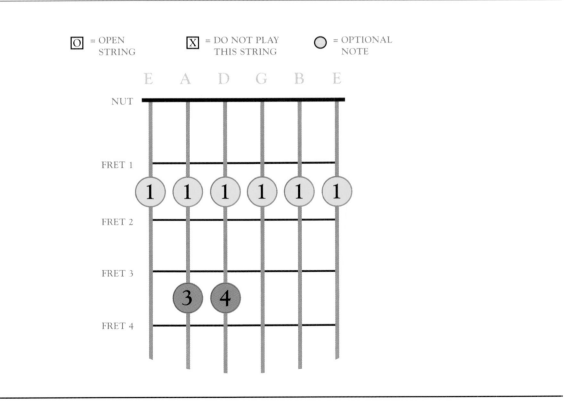

F#m7

Let your index finger play the 2nd fret of the bottom E string,
your middle finger the 2nd fret of the D string, your ring finger the 2nd fret of the G string
and your little finger the 2nd fret of the B string.

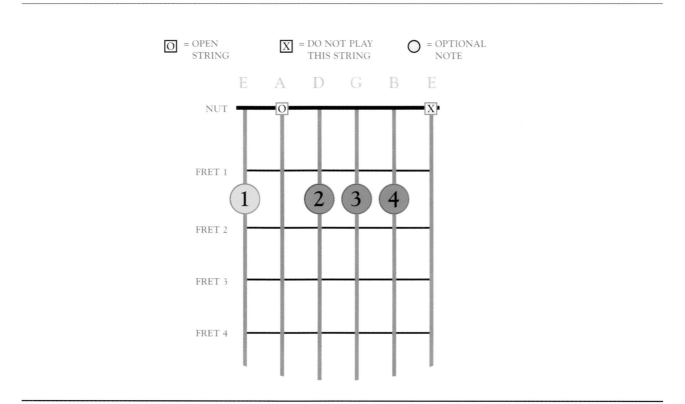

G

For the G chord your middle finger should play the 2nd fret of the A string,
while your ring finger plays the 3rd fret of the bottom E string
and your little finger plays the 3rd fret of the top E string.

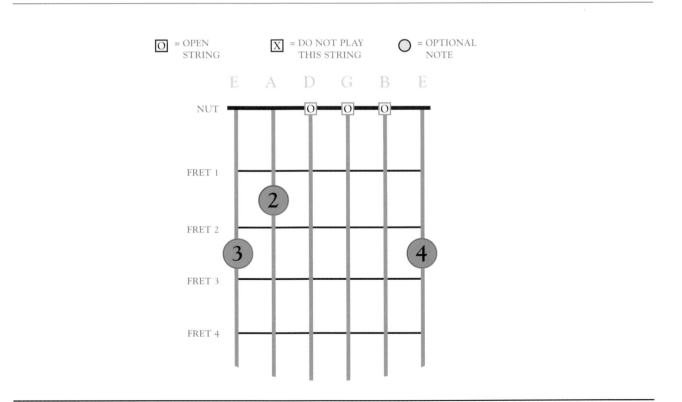

G (alt)

Let your index finger play the 2nd fret of the A string,
your middle finger the 3rd fret of the bottom E, your little finger the 3rd fret of the top E
and your ring finger the 3rd fret of the B string.

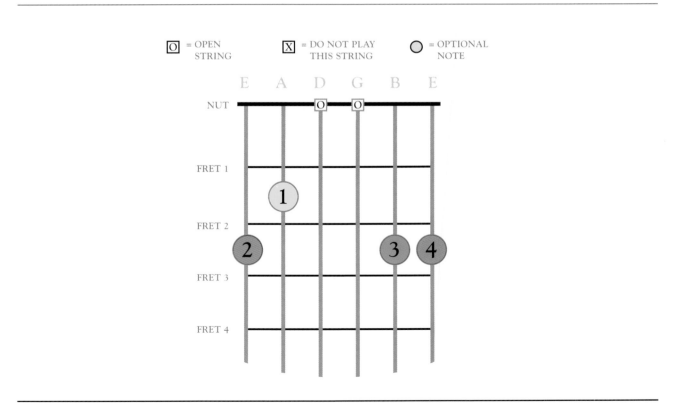

G Bar

Let your index finger play the 3rd fret of every string,
your middle finger the 4th fret of the G string, your ring finger the 5th fret of the A string
and your little finger the 5th fret of the D string.

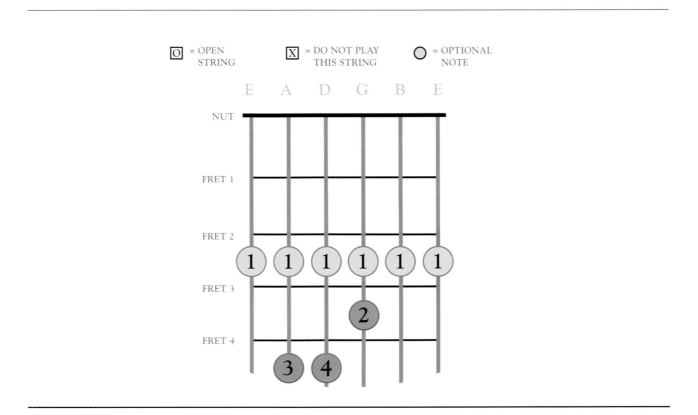

G7

Your index finger should play the 1st fret of the top E string,
your middle finger should play the 2nd fret of the A string
and your ring finger should play the 3rd fret of the bottom E string.

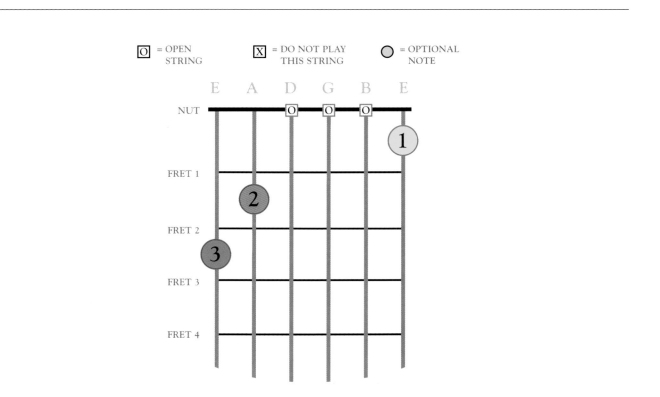

GM7

Using your index finger play the 2nd fret of the top E string,
while your middle finger plays the 2nd fret of the A string
and your ring finger plays the 3rd fret of the bottom E string.

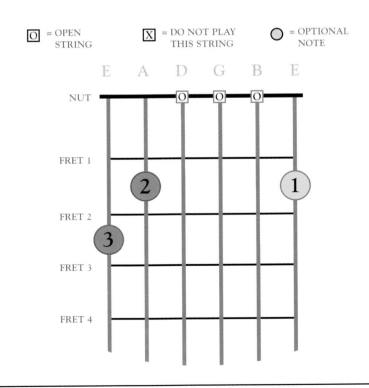

Gm

Let your index finger play the 5th fret of the D string,

while your middle finger plays the 6th fret of the top E string,

your ring finger the 7th fret of the G string and your little finger the 8th fret of the B string.

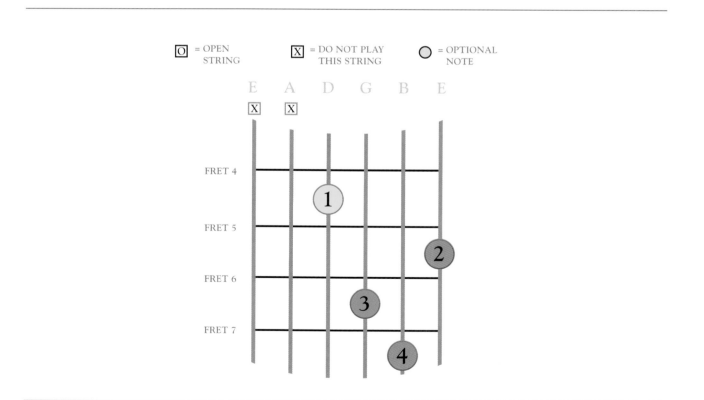

Gm (alt)

Using your index finger play the 3rd fret of all six strings,
while your ring finger should play the 5th fret of the A string
and your little finger should play the 5th fret of the D string.

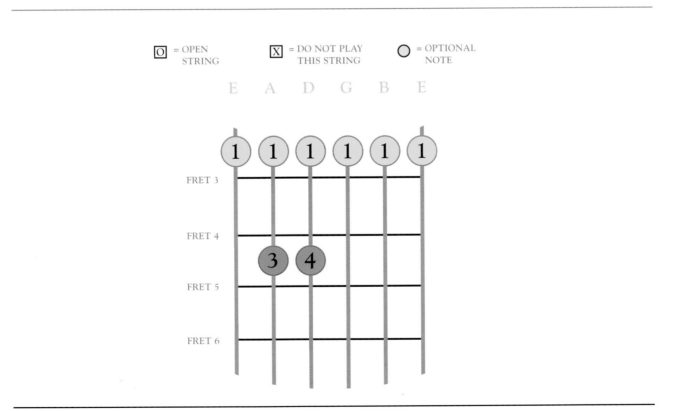

Gm Bar

Using your index finger play the 3rd fret of all six strings,
while your ring finger plays the 5th fret of the A string
and your little finger plays the 5th fret of the D string.

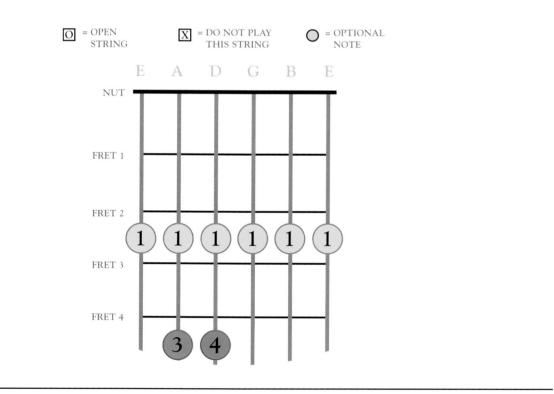

Gm7

Let your index finger play the 3rd fret of the bottom E string,
your middle finger the 3rd fret of the D string, your ring finger the 3rd fret of the G string
and your little finger the 3rd fret of the B string.

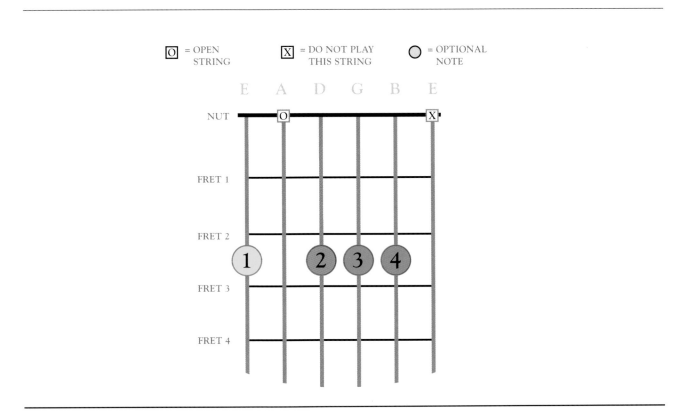

O = OPEN STRING   X = DO NOT PLAY THIS STRING   ○ = OPTIONAL NOTE

G6

Let your index finger play the 3rd fret of the top E string,
while your middle plays the 4th fret of the G string, your ring finger the 5th fret of the D string
and your little finger the 5th fret of the B string.

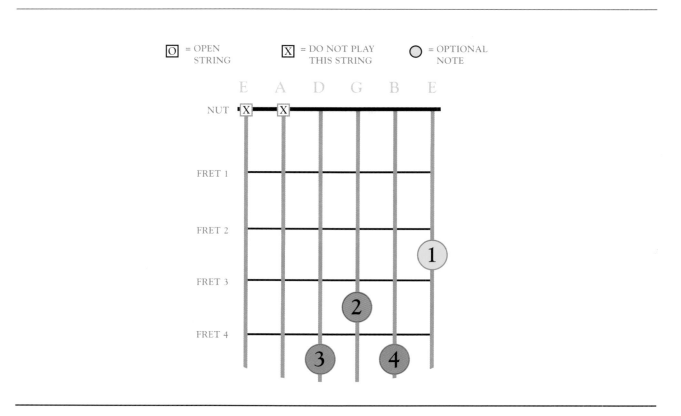

G9

Let your index finger play the 3rd fret of all six strings,
your middle finger the 4th fret of the G string, your ring finger the 5th fret of the A string
and your little finger the 5th fret of the top E string.

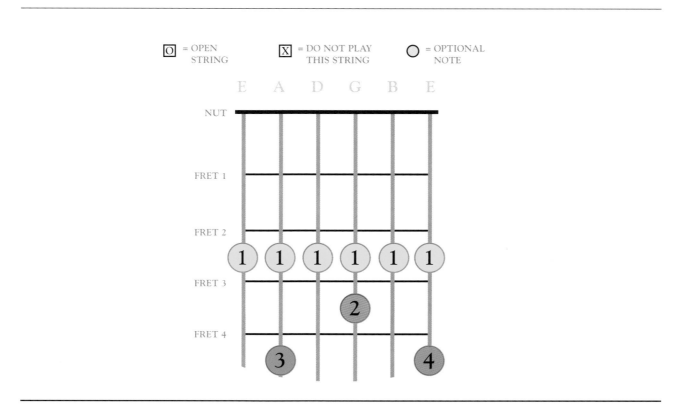

Index

Picture Credits
All photographs © Amber Books Ltd.